Norther Spai

MW00893729

2024-2025

Essential Tips for Exploring the Basque Country and Beyond

Lawrence J. Martinez

Copyright © 2024 Lawrence J. Martinez

All rights reserved. No part of this travel guide may be reproduced, stored in a retrieval system, or transmitted in any form or by any means, electronic, mechanical, photocopying, recording, or otherwise, without the prior written permission of the copyright holder, except for brief quotations in critical reviews or articles.

Overview Northern Spain Travel Guide 2024-2025

Welcome to your essential companion for exploring the enchanting regions of Northern Spain! This travel guide is designed to help you navigate the breathtaking landscapes, rich history, and vibrant culture that await you in this remarkable part of the country.

Chapter 1 introduces you to Northern Spain, delving into its timeless stories and cultural significance. You'll discover why 2024-2025 is the perfect time to visit, alongside intriguing facts and insights about the geography and climate of the region.

In **Chapter 2**, we cover essential travel planning, providing you with vital information on the best times to visit, entry requirements, budgeting tips, and what to pack to ensure a seamless journey.

Chapter 3 guides you on getting to Northern Spain, detailing international airports, transportation options, and eco-friendly travel choices to help reduce your carbon footprint.

Chapter 4 highlights top destinations, from the stunning coastlines of Galicia to the cultural hubs of the Basque Country. Explore must-see attractions like Santiago de Compostela and the picturesque villages of Asturias.

Where to stay is covered in **Chapter 5**, offering recommendations for luxury hotels and rural accommodations, as well as tips for securing the best options during peak travel seasons.

In **Chapter 6**, indulge in the rich gastronomy of Northern Spain. Discover must-try dishes, local seafood, and food tours that showcase the region's culinary delights, including wine and cider routes.

Chapter 7 invites you to partake in a variety of activities and outdoor experiences, whether you're hiking the Camino de Santiago, enjoying beach adventures, or participating in local festivals.

Chapter 8 is dedicated to shopping and souvenirs, guiding you on what to buy, where to find the best markets, and the unique crafts of Northern Spain.

For families, **Chapter 9** provides insights into kid-friendly attractions, educational activities, and tips for making the most of your travel with children.

Chapter 10 suggests exciting day trips and weekend getaways, ensuring you can explore nearby gems like the Rioja Wine Region and the picturesque lakes of Covadonga.

Finally, **Chapter 11** offers practical travel tips, including local etiquette, safety information, and valuable resources to enhance your journey.

As you turn the pages of this guide, prepare to embark on an unforgettable adventure through Northern Spain, filled with rich experiences, breathtaking views, and lasting memories. Safe travels!

Table of Contents

Chapter 1..11
Introduction.. 11
  A Land of History and Timeless Stories.. 11
  Why Visit Northern Spain in 2024-2025?......................14
  History and Culture.. 20
  Facts about Northern Spain...23
  Geography and Climate of Northern Spain...................28
Chapter 2..33
Essential Travel Planning..................................... 33
  Best Time to Visit Northern Spain.................................33
  Entry Requirement and Visa Information..................... 36
  Currency and Budgeting for Your Trip....................42
  What to Pack.. 49
  Staying Connected..51
Chapter 3...53
Getting there.. 53
  International Airports in Northern Spain...................... 53
  Getting Around Northern Spain.................................... 56
  Eco-Friendly Transportation Options........................... 63
Chapter 4...65
Top Destination in Northern Spain......................65
  Galicia..66
    Santiago de Compostela.. 66
    A Coruña... 75
    Rías Baixas... 82
  Asturias.. 89

Oviedo...90

Gijón.. 95

Picos de Europa.......................................101

Cantabria.. 107

Santander...108

Comillas and Santillana del Mar...................113

Cabárceno Nature Park....................... 119

Basque Country.................................. 124

Bilbao... 125

San Sebastián.................................. 131

Vitoria-Gasteiz...............................136

Navarra... 141

Pamplona.......................................142

Baztan Valley................................. 146

Chapter 5.. **152**

Where to Stay....................................**152**

Luxury Hotels in Northern Spain................. 152

Rural Stays Accommodations and Casas Rurales........ 158

Tips for Booking Accommodation During Peak Season163

Chapter 6.. **165**

Gastronomy and Culinary Experiences............... **165**

Must-Try Dishes in Northern Spain................ 166

Galician Seafood...168

Asturian Delights......................................169

Basque Cuisine..171

Navarra's Specialties................................ 172

Wine and Cider Routes...............................174

Best Markets and Food Tours.............................. 176
Vegetarian and Vegan Options.........................179

Chapter 7...181

Activities and Outdoor Experiences.................... 181

Hiking and Nature Walks.............................. 181
Camino de Santiago..................................... 182
Beaches and Coastal Adventures.................... 183
Surfing Spots.. 184
Hidden Coves and Family-Friendly Beaches.............185
Festival and Events..................................... 185
Wildlife Watching.. 190
Watersports..191

Chapter 8... 193

Shopping and Souvernirs............................193

What to Buy... 193
Best Shopping Streets and Markets........................... 196
Wine and Food Gifts.....................................199
Santiago's Craft Markets and Galician Pottery............ 202

Chapter 9..205

Family Travel in Northern Spain...................... 205

Kid-Friendly Destinations and Attractions..................206
Family Beaches and Parks............................209
Museums and Educational Activities for Children........ 211
Tips for Traveling with Kids.............................214

Chapter 10..217

Day Trips and Weekend Getaways......................217

From Bilbao: Rioja Wine Region and Gaztelugatxe...... 217

From Santiago de Compostela: Rías Baixas and Lugo.. 221

From San Sebastián: French Basque Country and Biarritz 223

From Oviedo: Cudillero and Covadonga Lakes.............226

Chapter 11... **230**

Practical Travel Tips...................................230

Local Etiquette and Cultural Do's and Don'ts...............230

Safety Tips and Emergency Contacts in Northern Spain.... 231

Basic Spanish Language for Tourists.........................235

Sustainable and Responsible Tourism in Northern Spain.. 237

Insider Tips from Locals for Traveling in Northern Spain. 240

Useful Websites and Travel Resources for Northern Spain 243

Conclusion..247

Chapter 1

Introduction

A Land of History and Timeless Stories

Imagine standing on the rugged cliffs of Northern Spain, with the crashing waves of the Atlantic Ocean behind you, and before you lies a landscape steeped in ancient stories, vibrant traditions, and a past that has shaped not only Spain but the world. Northern Spain isn't just a region; it's a living tapestry of history that draws travelers in with its tales of old kingdoms, brave explorers, and a culture deeply rooted in tradition.

Northern Spain has always been a crossroads of history. Long before it became a modern travel destination, it was home to some of the most important events in European history. Its story begins with ancient tribes like the Celts, who roamed the green valleys of Galicia, playing their haunting bagpipes, while in the mountains, the Romans left the zir marks as they marched through the region, building roads and bridges that stand to this day.

However, perhaps the most defining moment in Northern Spain's past came in the 8th century. Spain had been largely conquered by the Moors, except for the far north. In the remote mountains of Asturias, a small group of Christian warriors, led by a man named Pelayo, made their stand. The Battle of Covadonga fought in 722, marked the beginning of what would become the Reconquista, the centuries-long struggle to reclaim Spain from Moorish rule. This victory wasn't just a military triumph; it became a symbol of hope and resilience for the entire nation. Pelayo's tiny kingdom of Asturias eventually grew into the mighty kingdoms that would unite to form modern Spain.

But Northern Spain isn't all about battles and wars. It's also a land of pilgrimage and faith. For over a thousand years, millions of pilgrims have made their way across the region on the Camino de Santiago, or the Way of St. James, seeking spiritual renewal or simply a deeper connection to the world. This journey ends in Santiago de Compostela, where, according to legend, the remains of Saint James the Apostle are buried. The city's magnificent cathedral is a testament to faith and devotion, drawing visitors not just for its spiritual significance but for the breathtaking beauty of its architecture.

Another moment that captures the spirit of Northern Spain is the rise of the Basque culture, a culture so unique that its language, Euskara, is unlike any other in Europe. Even after centuries of change, the Basque people have managed to preserve their language, traditions, and identity. In cities like Bilbao, you can witness this blend of old and new, where the Guggenheim Museum, a marvel of modern art and architecture, stands alongside centuries-old markets and neighborhoods.

Northern Spain is where the past breathes in the present, and history isn't something you read about in books—it's something you experience. Whether you're walking along ancient Roman roads, standing in awe at the medieval cathedrals, or joining in the centuries-old festivals that continue to this day, the stories of Northern Spain will captivate you.

In this book, you'll not only explore the breathtaking landscapes and hidden gems of Northern Spain, but you'll also dive deep into the history that makes this region so extraordinary. It's more than just a travel destination—it's a place where the past and present are woven together, offering an unforgettable journey for anyone willing to discover its secrets.

Why Visit Northern Spain in 2024-2025?

Northern Spain offers an incredible blend of culture, history, natural beauty, and modern attractions that make it a must-visit destination, especially in 2024-2025. Unlike the more frequented southern parts of Spain, Northern Spain presents travelers with an experience that is rich in authenticity, away from the larger crowds, but full of hidden gems. Here's why visiting Northern Spain should be at the top of your list for the coming year:

Unspoiled Natural Beauty

Northern Spain is known as "Green Spain" for a reason. Its landscape is lush and vibrant, with rolling hills, rugged coastlines, and majestic mountains. In 2024-2025, travelers can expect even more opportunities to explore this stunning scenery, whether by hiking through the Picos de Europa National Park, surfing the waves along the Costa Verde, or simply enjoying the untouched beaches and quaint fishing villages.

The beauty of the countryside, especially in regions like Galicia and Asturias, is enhanced by the region's commitment to preserving its environment. Ecotourism has become a growing trend, with more sustainable travel options available for the environmentally conscious traveler.

Rich Cultural Heritage

Northern Spain is not just about natural landscapes; its cultural heritage is just as compelling. The Basque Country, Galicia, and Asturias all have unique languages, traditions, and festivals that bring their history to life. Whether it's experiencing the Running of the Bulls in Pamplona during San Fermín, attending the week-long Semana Grande festival in Bilbao, or witnessing the mystical pilgrimage of the Camino de Santiago, travelers in 2024-2025 will have a wealth of cultural experiences to enjoy.

In particular, the Camino de Santiago pilgrimage continues to draw visitors from around the world. In recent years, the trail has become more accessible, with new infrastructure catering to both seasoned pilgrims and casual travelers who want to explore part of this legendary route.

Culinary Paradise

For food lovers, Northern Spain offers an unmatched gastronomic experience. The region is known for its fresh seafood, world-class wines, and hearty dishes that are rooted in tradition. In 2024-2025, Northern Spain will continue to grow its reputation as a culinary hotspot, especially in cities like San Sebastián, which boasts more Michelin-starred restaurants per capita than anywhere else in the world.

From the pintxos (small, flavorful snacks) in the Basque Country to pulpo a la gallega (Galician-style octopus) in Galicia, your taste buds are in for an adventure. For those who love a good drink, don't miss the chance to try Asturian cider or take a tour of the Rioja wine region, which borders the Basque Country.

Historical Sites and Modern Marvels

Northern Spain is a place where history and modernity meet in perfect harmony. In Bilbao, for instance, the futuristic Guggenheim Museum contrasts beautifully with the traditional Casco Viejo (Old Town). The region is also home to medieval cathedrals, Roman bridges, and ancient fortresses that tell the story of Spain's rich past.

In 2024-2025, these historical sites are more accessible than ever, with updated tours and guides that make exploring them easy and informative. Whether you're visiting the Santiago de Compostela Cathedral or exploring the ancient caves of Altamira with prehistoric cave paintings, there's a new wave of modern resources to help you connect with Northern Spain's history.

Off the Beaten Path

While Southern Spain is well-known for its beaches and resorts, Northern Spain offers a quieter, more serene alternative for travelers seeking a more relaxed and less commercialized experience. In 2024-2025, the region's hidden villages, like Cudillero in Asturias or Comillas in Cantabria, will give visitors the chance to immerse themselves in local life. These smaller destinations are full of charm, often with fewer tourists, making it perfect for those who want to explore Spain's authentic culture.

Outdoor Adventures

Northern Spain is a playground for adventure seekers. Whether you enjoy hiking, skiing, surfing, or cycling, you'll find plenty to do here. The Picos de Europa mountains offer breathtaking trails for hikers, while the beaches of San Sebastián and Zarautz are ideal for surfers. In 2024-2025, the region is expected to further expand its adventure tourism offerings, with new trails and outdoor activities available for travelers of all experience levels.

In 2024-2025, Northern Spain offers an experience that is diverse, authentic, and deeply rooted in history and culture. Whether you're looking to soak in the region's natural beauty, indulge in its world-class cuisine, or delve into its rich cultural and historical heritage, Northern Spain has something for everyone. The coming years present the perfect opportunity to explore this less-traveled part of the country and create unforgettable memories.

History and Culture

Northern Spain is a region steeped in rich history and diverse cultures, each area distinct in its traditions and heritage. From ancient civilizations to medieval kingdoms, Northern Spain has played a pivotal role in shaping not only Spanish history but also that of Europe.

One of the earliest known inhabitants of Northern Spain were the Celts, whose influence can still be seen today, particularly in Galicia, where the sound of bagpipes and Celtic festivals remain an integral part of cultural life. The Romans arrived in the region around the 2nd century BC, bringing with them infrastructure, such as roads and bridges, many of which are still in use today. One notable example is the Roman Walls of Lugo, which have stood for nearly 2,000 years and remain remarkably well-preserved.

However, Northern Spain is perhaps most famous for its role in the Reconquista, the centuries-long effort to reclaim Spain from Moorish rule. In the 8th century, the small kingdom of Asturias became the starting point for this campaign. The victory at the Battle of Covadonga in 722, led by the Asturian king Pelayo, marked the first major triumph against the Moors, giving rise to a movement that would eventually lead to the unification of Spain.

Another major part of Northern Spain's cultural fabric is the Camino de Santiago, a pilgrimage route that has been walked by millions of people for over a thousand years. Ending at the Santiago de Compostela Cathedral in Galicia, where the remains of Saint James the Apostle are believed to be buried, this pilgrimage has shaped the spiritual and cultural identity of Northern Spain. Pilgrims come from around the world to walk this sacred path, seeking spiritual enlightenment or personal growth.

In the Basque Country, the unique Basque culture continues to thrive. The Basque language, Euskara, is unlike any other in Europe, and the region's long-standing traditions of independence and resilience are evident in its cultural festivals, cuisine, and vibrant communities. Cities like Bilbao offer a blend of old and new, with the iconic Guggenheim Museum representing modern innovation, while the streets are filled with traditional markets and pintxo bars.

Northern Spain's history and culture are a fascinating mix of ancient traditions, religious significance, and modern innovation, making it a destination where the past and present come together seamlessly.

Facts about Northern Spain

Green Spain: Northern Spain is often called "Green Spain" due to its lush landscapes, which stand in contrast to the drier, more arid regions of southern Spain. The area is known for its greenery, thanks to the frequent rainfall.

Unique Languages: In Northern Spain, multiple languages are spoken besides Spanish. Galician in

Galicia, Euskara (Basque) in the Basque Country, and Asturian in Asturias are recognized regional languages.

The Camino de Santiago: The Camino de Santiago, or Way of St. James, is one of the most famous pilgrimage routes in the world, attracting thousands of pilgrims each year who walk or cycle to the Santiago de Compostela Cathedral.

Santiago de Compostela: The Santiago de Compostela Cathedral in Galicia is believed to house the remains of Saint James the Apostle, making it one of the most important religious sites in Europe.

Reconquista Began Here: The Reconquista, the Christian campaign to reclaim Spain from Moorish rule, began in Northern Spain, with the first victory at the Battle of Covadonga in Asturias in 722 AD.

The Basque Country's Independence Movement: The Basque Country has a long history of striving for political and cultural autonomy, and its regional government enjoys significant autonomy under the Statute of Autonomy.

World-Class Cuisine: The Basque Country is a gastronomic powerhouse, with San Sebastián having more Michelin-starred restaurants per capita than any other city in the world. Pintxos, or small snacks, are a Basque specialty.

The Guggenheim Museum: Bilbao is home to the world-renowned Guggenheim Museum, a striking example of modern architecture that helped transform the city into a cultural hub.

Asturias' Natural Beauty: The Picos de Europa mountains in Asturias and Cantabria are some of the most breathtaking natural landscapes in Spain, ideal for hiking and wildlife spotting.

Celtic Heritage: Galicia has a strong Celtic heritage, with many cultural elements, such as music and festivals, reminiscent of the Celtic traditions of Ireland and Scotland.

Cider Tradition: Asturias is famous for its sidra (cider), which is poured from a height to aerate the drink. Visiting a sidrería, or cider house, is a must-do when in Asturias.

San Fermín Festival: The San Fermín Festival in Pamplona, Navarra, is world-famous for the Running of the Bulls, where people run alongside bulls through the city streets.

Natural Caves: The Altamira Caves in Cantabria are home to prehistoric cave paintings, often called the "Sistine Chapel of Paleolithic Art," with some of the earliest known examples of human art.

Traditional Paradores: Northern Spain is home to several Paradores, luxury hotels located in historical buildings such as castles, palaces, and monasteries, giving visitors a unique stay.

Festivals Galore: Northern Spain is home to numerous unique festivals, including the Semana Grande in Bilbao and San Sebastián, which feature concerts, bullfights, fireworks, and parades.

Beach Heaven: The northern coast of Spain, particularly in Cantabria and the Basque Country, offers some of the best surfing spots in Europe, including Zarautz and Mundaka.

Roman History: The city of Lugo in Galicia is encircled by fully intact Roman walls, which are a UNESCO World Heritage Site and a testament to the region's Roman past.

The Way of the Bear: Asturias is home to the Cantabrian brown bear, a protected species that can be seen in some parts of the region, particularly in the Somiedo Natural Park.

Political Autonomy: The Basque Country and Navarra are autonomous communities with their own parliaments and police forces. They also have fiscal autonomy, meaning they manage their own taxes.

Incredible Beaches: The Costa Verde (Green Coast) of Northern Spain offers stunning, unspoiled beaches, such as the famous Playa de las Catedrales in Galicia, which features dramatic rock formations.

These facts showcase Northern Spain's unique blend of historical significance, cultural richness, and natural beauty, making it a fascinating destination for travelers.

Geography and Climate of Northern Spain

Northern Spain is a region known for its striking landscapes, ranging from rugged coastlines to lush mountains and fertile valleys. Unlike the sun-drenched southern parts of Spain, Northern Spain is cooler and greener, thanks to its proximity to the Atlantic Ocean and the Bay of Biscay. The region is often referred to as "Green Spain" due to its abundant rainfall and lush vegetation, making it a stark contrast to the drier, Mediterranean climates found in other parts of the country.

Geography

Northern Spain spans several autonomous communities, including Galicia, Asturias, Cantabria, the

Basque Country, and Navarra, each with its distinct geography:

Galicia: Situated in the far northwest, Galicia boasts a dramatic coastline with numerous rias—deep, river-like inlets formed by submerged river valleys. Its interior is hilly and dotted with ancient forests, while its coastline features stunning cliffs and sandy beaches.

Asturias: Known for its mountain ranges, Asturias is home to the Picos de Europa, one of the most stunning natural parks in Spain. The region's geography is a mix of high mountains, deep valleys, and picturesque coastal towns.

Cantabria: Cantabria is sandwiched between Asturias and the Basque Country, offering a diverse geography of rolling hills, fertile plains, and dramatic coastal cliffs. Its inland areas are also mountainous, providing excellent hiking and skiing opportunities.

Basque Country: The Basque Country features both rugged mountains and a stunning coastline. The western parts are dominated by the Pyrenees

Mountains, while the northern coast is lined with pristine beaches, cliffs, and vibrant cities like Bilbao and San Sebastián.

Navarra: Navarra offers a mix of geographical features, from the towering Pyrenees in the north to the semi-arid plains in the south. It also has fertile river valleys that are perfect for agriculture.

Climate

Northern Spain's climate is heavily influenced by the Atlantic Ocean and the Bay of Biscay, giving the region a temperate maritime climate. This means it has milder summers and cooler winters than the rest of Spain. The climate is characterized by more frequent rainfall, especially in the winter months, which nourishes the lush, green landscapes.

Summer: Summers in Northern Spain are generally mild and pleasant, with average temperatures ranging from **60°F to 77°F (15°C to 25°C)**. Coastal areas remain cooler due to the Atlantic breeze, making it a great escape from the heat of southern Spain.

Winter: Winters are cooler, especially in the mountainous regions. Inland areas, particularly in Asturias and Navarra, can see snowfall, making them popular for winter sports. Average winter temperatures range from **40°F to 55°F (4°C to 13°C)**, though it can be colder in the mountains.

Rainfall: Rain is more frequent in Northern Spain than in other parts of the country, particularly in Galicia and the coastal regions. The region receives consistent rainfall throughout the year, with peaks in autumn and winter. The lush greenery of the region owes much to this regular rain, but it's also why travelers should always be prepared for sudden showers, even in the summer.

Microclimates

Thanks to its varied geography, Northern Spain also has numerous **microclimates**. Coastal areas, for instance, enjoy a milder climate, while the inland regions and highlands can experience more extreme weather conditions, including heavier rainfall and colder winters.

Overall, Northern Spain's diverse geography and temperate climate make it a perfect destination for those looking to enjoy both natural beauty and outdoor activities, without the intense heat found in other parts of Spain. Whether you're hiking in the Picos de Europa, relaxing on the beaches of the Basque Country, or exploring the valleys of Navarra, Northern Spain's geography and climate offer something for everyone.

Chapter 2

Essential Travel Planning

Best Time to Visit Northern Spain

The best time to visit Northern Spain largely depends on what kind of experience you're looking for. Whether you prefer outdoor activities, cultural events, or just enjoying the scenic beauty, Northern Spain offers something for every season. Here's a breakdown of the weather, seasons, and events to help you plan your trip.

Spring (March to May)

Spring is one of the best times to visit Northern Spain, as the weather is mild and the landscapes are lush and green, thanks to the winter rains. Average temperatures range from 50°F to 68°F (10°C to 20°C), making it perfect for hiking, exploring the countryside, and enjoying coastal walks. This is also the season for many local festivals, including Semana Santa (Holy Week) in

April, which is celebrated across the region with religious processions and events.

Summer (June to August)

Summer is the most popular time to visit, particularly for beach lovers and festival-goers. Temperatures are warm, averaging between 65°F and 77°F (18°C to 25°C), especially along the coast, making it a great time for water sports, sunbathing, and outdoor activities. San Sebastián and Zarautz are popular surfing spots during this time.

Summer is also when major events like the San Fermín Festival in Pamplona (July) and Semana Grande in Bilbao and San Sebastián (August) take place. These festivals draw large crowds, so book accommodations in advance if you plan to attend.

Autumn (September to November)

Autumn is another excellent time to visit, especially for those who want to avoid the summer crowds. The weather is cooler but still pleasant, with temperatures between 55°F and 70°F (13°C to 21°C). The fall foliage in regions like Asturias and Cantabria is stunning, making it ideal for hiking and nature trips.

Autumn also brings the cider harvest season in Asturias and Galicia's wine harvest festivals, giving visitors a chance to taste local specialties and join in the celebrations.

Winter (December to February)

Winter is the least popular time to visit due to colder weather, particularly in mountainous regions, where temperatures can drop to 40°F (4°C) or lower. However, if you enjoy skiing, the Picos de Europa offer excellent opportunities for winter sports. Additionally, Christmas markets and festivals like Carnival in February add a festive atmosphere to the cities.

The best time to visit Northern Spain depends on what you're looking for. Spring and autumn offer pleasant weather, fewer crowds, and beautiful natural scenery, while summer is ideal for beach lovers and festival-goers. Winter brings a quieter atmosphere with opportunities for winter sports and festive celebrations.

Entry Requirement and Visa Information

If you're planning to visit Northern Spain in 2024-2025, it's essential to understand the entry requirements and visa information. Below is a detailed guide to help you prepare for a smooth entry into Spain.

Entry for EU/EEA and Schengen Area Citizens

- **Who Needs a Visa?**
  Citizens from EU, EEA (European Economic Area), and Schengen Area countries **do not** need a visa to enter Spain, including Northern Spain, for any length of stay.
- **Passport Requirements:**
  EU/EEA and Schengen Area citizens can enter Spain with a valid passport or a national identity card.

- **Length of Stay:**
  No restrictions apply to the length of stay for citizens from these areas.
- **Travel Tip:**
  Always ensure your identity documents are up to date and valid for the duration of your stay.

Entry for Non-EU/EEA Citizens

- **Who Needs a Visa?**
  Citizens from certain non-EU/EEA countries, including the U.S., Canada, Australia, and New Zealand, **do not need a visa** for short stays of up to 90 days within 180 days. However, stays beyond 90 days require a visa.

ETIAS (European Travel Information and Authorization System):
Starting in **2025**, travelers from visa-exempt countries (such as the U.S. and Canada) will need to apply for **ETIAS** authorization before entering Spain. ETIAS is a mandatory travel authorization similar to the ESTA system in the U.S.

- ETIAS Website: https://etias.com
- **Application Cost:** Approximately €7, valid for multiple entries over 3 years.

Passport Requirements:

Non-EU citizens must have a passport that is valid for at least 3 months beyond the date of their intended departure from the Schengen area. The passport should have been issued within the last 10 years.

Length of Stay:

Non-EU visitors can stay for **up to 90 days** within 180 days without a visa under the Schengen Agreement. For stays longer than 90 days, a visa is required.

Visa Types for Longer Stays

If you plan to stay longer than 90 days, you will need to apply for one of the following visas:

- **Tourist/Short-Stay Visa (Schengen Visa):** Required for citizens of countries not exempt under the Schengen agreement for short stays of up to 90 days.

- **Long-Stay Visa:**
  Required for stays longer than 90 days. This visa may be necessary for students, workers, or those relocating to Spain for extended periods. Applications should be submitted at the Spanish consulate in your home country.

- **Work and Study Visas:**
  For those planning to work or study in Northern Spain, a work or student visa is required. Applications should be submitted through the Spanish embassy or consulate in your home country.
  Work Visa Information:
  https://extranjeros.inclusion.gob.es/es/index.html
  Study Visa Information:
  https://www.exteriores.gob.es/en/ServiciosAlCiudadano/Paginas/EmbajadasConsulados.aspx

Travel to Spain with Children

- **Parental Consent:**
  If a minor is traveling to Northern Spain with only one parent or without their legal guardian, some countries require an official consent letter from the other parent or guardian. It's best to check with your airline and country of origin for specific requirements.

- **Travel Tip:**
  Always carry the child's birth certificate and consent documents to avoid complications at border control.

Customs and Border Control

- **Permitted Goods:**
  When entering Spain, EU citizens can bring goods without paying additional duties. For non-EU citizens, goods such as alcohol, tobacco, and other items may be subject to certain limits.

- **Prohibited Items:**
Check with the **Spanish Customs Office** for a full list of prohibited and restricted items: https://www.agenciatributaria.es/

Health and Travel Insurance

- **Health Insurance:**
Travelers are advised to have comprehensive health insurance that covers medical treatment in Spain. For EU citizens, the **European Health Insurance Card (EHIC)** or the **Global Health Insurance Card (GHIC)** for UK citizens provides access to state healthcare in Spain.
EHIC/GHIC Information: https://tinyurl.com/3jpcd3cd
- **Travel Insurance:**
It's recommended that all travelers purchase travel insurance covering trip cancellations, lost luggage, and unexpected delays, particularly if

traveling during peak seasons or events like **San Fermín**.

By following these guidelines and being aware of the entry requirements, you'll ensure a smooth and hassle-free journey to Northern Spain. Always check official websites and consulate offices for the most up-to-date information regarding visas and entry policies.

Currency and Budgeting for Your Trip

Currency in Northern Spain

- **Currency**: Spain uses the **Euro (€)**, which is the official currency across the country, including Northern Spain. The Euro is divided into 100 cents. Commonly used coins are 1, 2, 5, 10, 20, and 50 cents, as well as 1€ and 2€ coins. Banknotes come in denominations of 5€, 10€, 20€, 50€, 100€, 200€, and 500€, though higher denominations (100€ and above) are less commonly accepted in smaller shops and restaurants.

- **Currency Code**: EUR
- **Symbol**: €
- **Where to Exchange Currency**:
  - **Airports**: Currency exchange services are available at major international airports in Northern Spain such as **Bilbao, Santiago de Compostela**, and **Santander.**
  - **Banks**: Banks in Northern Spain offer currency exchange, though they may have limited operating hours, especially on weekends.
  - **ATMs**: The most convenient way to get local currency is to withdraw money from an ATM. ATMs are widely available in cities and towns across Northern Spain, and most accept international cards such as **Visa, MasterCard**, and **Maestro**. Check with your bank before traveling to ensure your

card will work abroad and ask about any potential withdrawal fees.

- **Tip**: If you're withdrawing money from an ATM, select the option to be charged in **Euros** rather than your home currency to avoid hidden conversion fees.

Budgeting

The cost of travel in Northern Spain can vary depending on the type of trip you're planning. Below are estimates to help you budget for different levels of travel: budget, mid-range, and luxury.

Budget Traveler (Backpacking or Budget Travel)

- **Accommodation**: €25 - €50 per night (Hostels, budget hotels, or rural guesthouses)
- **Meals**: €10 - €20 per day (Local restaurants, cafés, and street food)
- **Transportation**: €10 - €20 per day (Buses, local trains, and walking)

- **Attractions**: €10 - €20 per day (Free or low-cost attractions such as museums, parks, and cathedrals)

Daily Budget: €45 - €100 per day

Travel Tips for Budget Travelers:

- **Accommodation**: Stay in hostels or **casas rurales** (rural guesthouses), which are affordable and give you a local experience. Consider staying in **albergues** if you're walking the **Camino de Santiago**, as they are inexpensive.
- **Meals**: Eat at **menú del día** restaurants that offer a set three-course meal for a fixed price, usually around €10 - €15. You can also find affordable pintxos bars in the Basque Country.
- **Transport**: Use public buses or regional trains. Cities like **Bilbao** and **Oviedo** have good public transport networks.

Mid-Range Traveler (Comfortable Travel)

- **Accommodation**: €70 - €120 per night (Mid-range hotels, boutique hotels, or apartments)
- **Meals**: €20 - €40 per day (Mid-range restaurants, including some higher-end places for dinner)
- **Transportation**: €20 - €40 per day (Trains, taxis, or car rentals)
- **Attractions**: €20 - €40 per day (Entry fees to museums, guided tours, etc.)

Daily Budget: €120 - €200 per day

Travel Tips for Mid-Range Travelers:

- **Accommodation**: Look for **boutique hotels** or **paradores** (luxury hotels in historical buildings) for a memorable stay without breaking the bank.
- **Meals**: Consider trying **pintxos** in the Basque Country or enjoying a seafood feast in **Galicia**.

For lunch, many restaurants offer **menú del día** at a good price.

- **Transport**: Rent a car if you're planning to explore rural areas or drive between regions, though public transport is more economical within cities.

Luxury Traveler (High-End Travel)

- **Accommodation**: €150 - €500 per night (Luxury hotels, paradores, or 5-star resorts)
- **Meals**: €50 - €150 per day (High-end dining, Michelin-starred restaurants, exclusive wine-tasting experiences)
- **Transportation**: €50 - €100 per day (Private transport, luxury car rentals, or first-class train tickets)
- **Attractions**: €40 - €100 per day (Private tours, premium experiences like wine tastings or sailing trips)

Daily Budget: €250 - €700 per day

Travel Tips for Luxury Travelers:

- **Accommodation**: Stay in luxury **paradores** or high-end hotels. Some paradores are located in castles or monasteries, offering a unique and luxurious experience.
- **Meals**: Dine at Michelin-starred restaurants, especially in **San Sebastián**, which is known for its culinary excellence. A meal at a top restaurant like **Arzak** or **Akelarre** can be a highlight of your trip.
- **Transport**: Book private transfers or hire a luxury car with a driver to explore the region at your leisure.

What to Pack

Clothing

- Lightweight jacket (for cool evenings)

- Raincoat or waterproof jacket (rain is common, especially in spring and autumn)
- Comfortable walking shoes (for city tours and hikes)
- Sandals or sneakers (for warmer weather and beach visits)
- Layers (sweaters, long-sleeve shirts for changing temperatures)
- T-shirts and light clothing for summer
- Warmer clothes (scarf, gloves, hat for winter trips or mountain areas)

Accessories

- Travel umbrella (compact, for sudden rain showers)
- Sunglasses and sunscreen (even during cooler months)
- Hat or cap (sun protection during hikes and beach days)
- Backpack (for day trips and hiking)

Documents

- Passport/ID
- Travel Insurance
- Copies of important documents (in case of loss)
- ETIAS (for visa-exempt travelers from 2025)

Tech and Gadgets

- Phone charger and portable battery pack
- Plug adapter (Spain uses **Type C** and **F** plugs, 230V)
- Camera or smartphone for photos

This list covers the basics and ensures you're ready for the varying climate and activities that Northern Spain offers.

Staying Connected

Staying connected in Northern Spain is easy with multiple options for SIM cards and internet access:

SIM Cards:

- Local SIM cards are available from major providers like **Movistar**, **Vodafone**, and **Orange**. You can purchase them at airports, phone shops, or convenience stores.
- **Prepaid plans** are ideal for tourists, offering data, calls, and texts. Plans typically range from **€10 to €30**, depending on the amount of data.
- Ensure your phone is **unlocked** before purchasing a SIM card.

Internet Access:

- **Wi-Fi** is widely available in hotels, cafes, and public areas like airports and city centers. Some rural areas may have limited access, so plan accordingly.
- If you need constant internet access, consider renting a **portable Wi-Fi device** (pocket Wi-Fi) for unlimited data, which can be shared across multiple devices.

By using a local SIM card or Wi-Fi, you can stay connected throughout your trip.

Chapter 3

Getting there

Northern Spain is well-connected by various modes of transportation, making it easy for travelers from around the world to reach this captivating region. Whether you prefer flying into one of the region's international airports, taking scenic train rides through the Spanish countryside, or driving along its beautiful coastal roads, there are multiple options to suit your travel preferences. In this section, we'll explore the best ways to reach Northern Spain, ensuring a smooth and enjoyable journey as you embark on your adventure.

International Airports in Northern Spain

Bilbao Airport (BIO)

- **Address**: 48180 Loiu, Bizkaia, Spain
- **Website**: www.aena.es/en/bilbao.html

- **Contact**: +34 913 211 000
- **Airlines**: Serves major airlines such as **Iberia, Vueling, Lufthansa, KLM, British Airways**, and **Air France**, offering flights to Europe and beyond.
- **Amenities**: Free Wi-Fi, duty-free shops, restaurants, car rentals, VIP lounges, and medical services.
- **Services**: 24/7 information desk, luggage storage, ATMs, currency exchange, and accessible services for travelers with reduced mobility.

Santiago de Compostela Airport (SCQ)

- **Address**: Lavacolla, 15820 Santiago de Compostela, A Coruña, Spain
- **Website**: https://www.aena.es/en/santiago-rosalia-de-cast ro.html
- **Contact**: +34 913 211 000

- **Airlines**: Connects with **Iberia, Ryanair, EasyJet, Vueling,** and **Aer Lingus** for European destinations.
- **Amenities**: Duty-free shops, cafés, car rentals, free Wi-Fi, and VIP lounges.
- **Services**: Medical assistance, accessible services, luggage assistance, and information desks.

Santander Airport (SDR)

- **Address**: Camargo, 39600, Cantabria, Spain
- **Website**: https://www.aena.es/en/seve-ballesteros-santander.html
- **Contact**: +34 913 211 000
- **Airlines**: Offers flights with **Ryanair, Vueling,** and **Iberia** to key European destinations.
- **Amenities**: Duty-free shops, restaurants, car hire services, and Wi-Fi access.
- **Services**: Tourist information, disabled access, and childcare facilities.

These airports serve as the main gateways to Northern Spain, providing easy access and a range of amenities for travelers.

Getting Around Northern Spain

Getting around Northern Spain is both convenient and enjoyable, thanks to its efficient public transportation systems, well-maintained roads, and scenic routes. Whether you prefer traveling by train, bus, or car, Northern Spain offers a variety of options that cater to different types of travelers. Below, we'll explore the best ways to navigate the region and ensure a smooth, comfortable experience.

Public Transportation

Northern Spain has an extensive public transportation network, making it easy to travel between cities and within local areas. The most common forms of public transport include **buses**, **trains**, **trams**, and **ferries**.

- **Buses**: Buses are the most commonly used form of public transportation in Northern Spain. Cities like **Bilbao**, **Santander**, and **Oviedo** have well-organized bus networks that cover urban areas as well as surrounding towns. **ALSA** is a major bus operator offering long-distance and intercity routes.
    - **Fares**: A typical bus fare within a city costs around €1.20 to €2.50, depending on the city. Long-distance bus trips may cost between €10 and €30.
    - **How to Purchase Tickets**: Tickets can be purchased at bus stations, on the bus, or through apps like **ALSA**. Multi-trip passes are available in most cities for frequent travelers.
- **Trains**: Spain's **RENFE** railway network offers efficient, comfortable train services across Northern Spain. **Cercanías** trains operate in local regions like the Basque Country, Asturias, and Cantabria, while **long-distance trains**

connect cities like **Bilbao, Oviedo**, and **Santiago de Compostela**.

- ○ **Fares**: Local train fares typically start from €1.50, while long-distance tickets may range from €20 to €60 depending on the distance and class.
- ○ **How to Purchase Tickets**: Tickets can be bought at stations, ticket machines, or online via the **RENFE** website or app. Early booking is recommended for long-distance routes, especially during peak seasons.
- **Trams and Ferries**: Some cities, like **Bilbao**, have tram systems that connect key areas, while coastal cities like **Santander** offer ferry services for short trips across bays or between towns.

Tips for Public Transportation:

- Most ticket machines and transport apps have English language options.

- Maps are available at stations, and apps like **Moovit** or **Google Maps** help plan routes in real time.

Taxis and Ridesharing Services

Taxis are widely available in cities and towns across Northern Spain, making them a convenient option for short trips or late-night transportation.

- **How to Hail a Taxi**: Taxis can be flagged down on the street or found at designated taxi ranks. You can also call for one, or use a taxi app like **Free Now** to book a ride.
- **Typical Fares**: Taxi fares start with a base rate of about €3, with an additional charge of approximately €1.10 per kilometer. Fares increase slightly at night or during public holidays.
- **Tips for Using Taxis**: It's common to round up the fare as a tip. Always ensure the meter is

running or agree on a price before starting your trip.

- **Ridesharing Services**: Apps like **Uber** and **Cabify** operate in many cities in Northern Spain.
  - **How to Use**: Download the app, register, and enter your payment details. It's an easy and safe way to get around, and drivers are generally well-rated.
  - **Safety Tips**: Verify the driver's identity and car plate number through the app before entering the vehicle.

Rental Cars and Driving

Renting a car is ideal for exploring Northern Spain's scenic countryside and remote areas that may not be accessible by public transport.

- **Rental Process**: Major rental companies like **Hertz**, **Avis**, and **Europcar** operate in cities and airports across the region.

- Requirements: You must be at least 21 years old (age may vary by company) and hold a valid driver's license. An international driver's permit may be required for non-EU travelers.
- Insurance: Basic insurance is usually included, but it's advisable to get full coverage for peace of mind.

- **Driving Conditions**: Roads in Northern Spain are well-maintained, but be prepared for narrow, winding roads in rural or mountainous areas.
  - Parking: Parking is available in cities but may be limited to busy areas. Use public parking garages or designated street parking zones.
  - Toll Roads: Some highways, like the **AP-8** in the Basque Country, are toll roads, so carry some change or be ready to use a credit card.

Safety and Security Tips

- Be cautious with your belongings in crowded areas, particularly on public transport.
- Use official taxi ranks or ridesharing apps for a safe travel experience.
- In case of emergencies, dial **112** for immediate assistance.

Local Etiquette and Customs

When using public transportation, it's polite to offer your seat to the elderly or disabled passengers. Tipping taxi drivers is appreciated but not required. Always queue for buses and taxis in an orderly manner.

For further transportation information, visit [https://www.renfe.com/] or check local tourist offices for route maps and schedules.

Eco-Friendly Transportation Options

Northern Spain offers a range of eco-friendly transportation options, making it easier for travelers to reduce their environmental impact while exploring the region.

Public Transport: Buses and trains are highly efficient and environmentally friendly. The RENFE trains, especially the high-speed AVE lines, are energy-efficient and run on clean energy sources

Biking: Cities like San Sebastián and Bilbao have extensive bike lanes, making cycling a green and healthy option. Many cities offer bike-sharing programs like Bilbao Bizi, providing short-term rentals for easy urban exploration.

Electric Vehicles: Renting electric cars is an increasingly popular option, with charging stations available in many cities and along major highways. Companies like Europcar offer electric and hybrid vehicle rentals.

Walking: Northern Spain's pedestrian-friendly cities and scenic hiking routes, including the Camino de Santiago, encourage walking as a zero-carbon way to explore.

By choosing these options, travelers can explore Northern Spain while minimizing their carbon footprint.

Chapter 4

Top Destination in Northern Spain

If you're looking for a destination that combines breathtaking natural beauty, rich history, and vibrant culture, Northern Spain is the place for you. Whether you want to explore the scenic coasts of **Galicia** and **Asturias**, dive into the modern wonders of **Bilbao**, or savor the incredible food scene in **San Sebastián**, this region has something for everyone. Picture yourself hiking through the stunning **Picos de Europa**, or experiencing the thrill of the **San Fermín Festival** in **Pamplona**. Northern Spain is packed with charming villages, famous landmarks, and traditions that make every visit unforgettable.

Galicia

If you're looking for a destination that combines stunning landscapes, rich history, and authentic culture,

Galicia is the perfect spot. Nestled in the northwest corner of Spain, this region is known for its lush green hills, dramatic coastlines, and the world-famous **Camino de Santiago** pilgrimage. Whether you want to explore the historic city of **Santiago de Compostela**, relax on the serene beaches of the **Rías Baixas**, or taste some of Spain's freshest seafood, Galicia has something for everyone. Its Celtic roots, traditional music, and welcoming atmosphere make it a destination that feels both ancient and alive.

Santiago de Compostela

Santiago de Compostela is a city rich in history and the spiritual heart of the **Camino de Santiago** pilgrimage. The stunning **Santiago de Compostela Cathedral** is a must-see, along with the charming **Old Town** and the lively **Praza do Obradoiro**, all offering a unique cultural and historical experience.

Santiago de Compostela Cathedral

The Final Destination of the Camino de Santiago

The **Santiago de Compostela Cathedral** is the crown jewel of the city and a UNESCO World Heritage Site. Here are the top things you can do at this breathtaking landmark:

Visit the Tomb of Saint James

- **Description**: Pay your respects at the tomb of Saint James, located in the crypt beneath the main altar.
- **Location**: Inside the Cathedral, Praza do Obradoiro.
- **How to get there**: Reach the Cathedral through the main square, **Praza do Obradoiro**.
- **Opening Hours**: 7:00 AM – 8:30 PM daily.
- **Entry Fee**: Free for worship; donations welcome.

Attend the Pilgrim's Mass

- **Description**: Experience the **Botafumeiro** incense swing and the spiritual Pilgrim's Mass.
- **Location**: Inside the Cathedral.
- **Opening Hours**: Pilgrim's Mass is held at 12:00 PM daily.
- **Entry Fee**: Free.

Climb the Cathedral Roof

- **Description**: Take a guided tour of the Cathedral's rooftop for panoramic views of Santiago.
- **Location**: Access through the main entrance.
- **Opening Hours**: 10:00 AM – 8:00 PM.
- **Entry Fee**: €12.
- **Website**: www.catedraldesantiago.es

Explore the Cathedral Museum

- **Description**: Discover centuries of history, art, and relics housed within the Cathedral Museum.
- **Location**: Inside the Cathedral complex.
- **Opening Hours**: 9:00 AM – 8:00 PM.

- **Entry Fee**: €6.
- **Contact**: +34 981 569 327, info@catedraldesantiago.es.

Praza do Obradoiro

Historic Square at the Heart of the City

Praza do Obradoiro is the vibrant heart of Santiago de Compostela, surrounded by stunning architecture and historical significance. Here are the top things to do in this iconic square:

Admire the Cathedral

- **Description**: Marvel at the stunning façade of the Santiago de Compostela Cathedral, a masterpiece of Romanesque architecture.
- **Location**: Praza do Obradoiro, Santiago de Compostela.
- **How to Get There**: Easily accessible by foot from anywhere in the Old Town.

- **Opening Hours**: Open 7:00 AM – 8:30 PM daily.
- **Entry Fee**: Free for worship; donations welcome.
- **Website**: www.catedraldesantiago.es

Visit the Hostal dos Reis Católicos

- **Description**: Explore this historic building, now a Parador, that once served as a hospital for pilgrims.
- **Location**: Praza do Obradoiro, Santiago de Compostela.
- **How to Get There**: Located directly on the square.
- **Opening Hours**: 24/7 for guests; restaurant hours vary.
- **Website**: www.parador.es

Enjoy the Atmosphere

- **Description**: Relax on the steps of the square, soaking in the lively atmosphere and street performances.

- **Location**: Praza do Obradoiro.
- **How to Get There**: Simply walk into the square.
- **Opening Hours**: Open 24/7.
- **Entry Fee**: Free.

Take Photos of the Surrounding Architecture

- **Description**: Capture the beautiful surroundings, including the **Palacio de Rajoy** and the **Colegio de San Jerónimo**.
- **Location**: Throughout Praza do Obradoiro.
- **How to Get There**: Explore the square on foot.
- **Opening Hours**: Open 24/7.
- **Entry Fee**: Free.

Enjoy your time in Praza do Obradoiro, where history and culture come alive!

Old Town

UNESCO World Heritage Site with Medieval Architecture

The **Old Town of Santiago de Compostela** is a treasure trove of medieval architecture and vibrant culture. Here are the top things to do in this historic area:

Visit the Santiago de Compostela Cathedral

- **Description**: The iconic cathedral is the focal point of the Old Town, famous for its stunning Romanesque façade and the tomb of Saint James.
- **Location**: Praza do Obradoiro, Santiago de Compostela.
- **How to Get There**: Centrally located; easily accessible on foot.
- **Opening Hours**: 7:00 AM – 8:30 PM daily.
- **Entry Fee**: Free for worship; donations appreciated.
- **Website**: www.catedraldesantiago.es

Explore Plaza de la Quintana

- **Description**: This historic square offers beautiful views and serves as a gathering place for locals and visitors alike.
- **Location**: Near the Cathedral, Santiago de Compostela.
- **How to Get There**: A short walk from the Cathedral.
- **Opening Hours**: Open 24/7.
- **Entry Fee**: Free.

Stroll Along Calle del Franco

- **Description**: Famous for its bustling atmosphere, this street is lined with restaurants and tapas bars where you can enjoy local cuisine.
- **Location**: Calle del Franco, Santiago de Compostela.
- **How to Get There**: Accessible by foot from the Cathedral.
- **Opening Hours**: Varies by establishment; typically from noon to late evening.
- **Entry Fee**: Free to explore; dining costs vary.

- **Visit the Museum of the Galician People**
- **Description**: Discover Galician culture and traditions through artifacts and exhibits.
- **Location**: Rúa de Revolta, 1, Santiago de Compostela.
- **How to Get There**: A short walk from the Cathedral.
- **Opening Hours**: 10:00 AM – 8:00 PM, closed Mondays.
- **Entry Fee**: €3.
- **Website**: www.museogalegodepobo.com

Enjoy wandering through the Old Town, where every corner reveals a piece of Santiago's rich history!

A Coruña

Maritime Charm and Modern Living

Tower of Hercules

The World's Oldest Functioning Lighthouse

The **Tower of Hercules** in A Coruña is a UNESCO World Heritage Site and a must-visit for its historical significance and stunning coastal views. Here are the top things you can do at this iconic landmark:

Climb the Tower

- **Description**: Ascend the 234 steps to the top for breathtaking panoramic views of the Atlantic Ocean and A Coruña.
- **Location**: Avenida de Navarra, A Coruña.
- **How to Get There**: Accessible by bus (Line 3) or a short taxi ride from the city center.
- **Opening Hours**: 10:00 AM – 8:00 PM (April to September); 10:00 AM – 6:00 PM (October to March).
- **Entry Fee**: €3.

Explore the Surrounding Park

- **Description**: Enjoy the beautiful gardens and walking paths around the tower, ideal for a stroll.
- **Location**: Parque de la Torre, A Coruña.

- **How to Get There**: Located adjacent to the tower; easily accessible on foot.
- **Opening Hours**: Open 24/7.
- **Entry Fee**: Free.

Visit the Interpretation Center

- **Description**: Learn about the history and significance of the Tower through informative displays and exhibits.
- **Location**: Next to the Tower of Hercules.
- **Opening Hours**: 10:00 AM – 7:00 PM (April to September); 10:00 AM – 5:00 PM (October to March).
- **Entry Fee**: Free.

Enjoy your visit to the Tower of Hercules, where history and stunning views come together!

Riazor Beach

Popular Beach with Promenade and Water Sports

Riazor Beach in A Coruña is a vibrant destination perfect for sunbathing, water sports, and enjoying local culture. Here are the top things you can do at this beautiful beach:

Relax on the Beach

- **Description**: Enjoy sunbathing on the sandy shores, perfect for families and solo travelers alike.
- **Location**: Avenida de la Habana, A Coruña.
- **How to Get There**: Easily accessible by bus (Lines 1 and 3) or a short walk from the city center.
- **Opening Hours**: Open 24/7.
- **Entry Fee**: Free.

Water Sports

- **Description**: Try your hand at various water sports, including surfing, paddleboarding, and windsurfing. Rentals are available nearby.
- **Location**: Riazor Beach area.

- **How to Get There**: Head to the beach; rental kiosks are located along the promenade.
- **Opening Hours**: Varies by season; generally from 10:00 AM to 7:00 PM.
- **Entry Fee**: Prices vary by activity.

Promenade Stroll

- **Description**: Take a leisurely walk along the picturesque promenade, lined with cafés and restaurants offering local cuisine.
- **Location**: Promenade adjacent to Riazor Beach.
- **How to Get There**: Accessible directly from the beach.
- **Opening Hours**: Open 24/7.
- **Entry Fee**: Free.

Enjoy your time at Riazor Beach, where relaxation and adventure meet!

Marina District

A Lively Area for Dining, Shopping, and Nightlife

The **Marina District** in A Coruña is a vibrant hub that combines stunning waterfront views with a lively atmosphere. Here are the top things you can do in this exciting area:

Dine at Waterfront Restaurants

- **Description**: Enjoy fresh seafood and traditional Galician dishes at numerous restaurants lining the marina.
- **Location**: Avenida de la Marina, A Coruña.
- **How to Get There**: A short walk from the city center or Riazor Beach.
- **Opening Hours**: Typically from 1:00 PM to 11:00 PM.
- **Entry Fee**: Free; dining costs vary.

Shop in Local Boutiques

- **Description**: Explore charming shops and boutiques offering local crafts, fashion, and souvenirs.

- **Location**: Throughout the Marina District.
- **How to Get There**: Easily accessible on foot from nearby attractions.
- **Opening Hours**: Generally from 10:00 AM to 8:00 PM.
- **Entry Fee**: Free.

Enjoy the Nightlife

- **Description**: Experience the vibrant nightlife with bars and clubs featuring live music and entertainment.
- **Location**: Marina District, particularly around the waterfront.
- **How to Get There**: Walkable from various points in the district.
- **Opening Hours**: Varies by venue; typically open until 2:00 AM or later.
- **Entry Fee**: Free; cover charges may apply at some venues.

Immerse yourself in the lively atmosphere of the Marina District, where dining, shopping, and nightlife come together for an unforgettable experience!

Rías Baixas

Coastal Retreats and Wine Routes

Playa de la Lanzada

Scenic Beach Along the Atlantic Coast

Playa de la Lanzada is one of Galicia's most stunning beaches, perfect for sunbathing, swimming, and water sports. Here are the top things you can do at this beautiful beach:

Relax on the Sandy Shores

- **Description**: Enjoy the expansive golden sands and crystal-clear waters, ideal for sunbathing and picnicking.

- **Location**: Playa de la Lanzada, Sanxenxo, Pontevedra.
- **How to Get There**: Accessible by car or bus from nearby towns like Sanxenxo and O Grove.
- **Opening Hours**: Open 24/7.
- **Entry Fee**: Free.

Water Sports and Surfing

- **Description**: Try your hand at surfing, paddleboarding, or windsurfing with equipment rentals available on-site.
- **Location**: Beachfront area.
- **How to Get There**: Head to the beach; rental kiosks are located along the shore.
- **Opening Hours**: Varies by season; generally from 10:00 AM to 7:00 PM.
- **Entry Fee**: Prices vary by activity.

Explore Nearby Dunes and Nature

- **Description**: Walk through the nearby sand dunes and natural landscapes, perfect for photography and birdwatching.
- **Location**: Adjacent to Playa de la Lanzada.
- **How to Get There**: Easily accessible from the beach.
- **Opening Hours**: Open 24/7.
- **Entry Fee**: Free.

Enjoy your time at Playa de la Lanzada, where natural beauty and adventure await!

Albariño Wine Vineyards

Wine Tastings and Tours

The **Albariño Wine Vineyards** in the Rías Baixas region of Galicia are renowned for producing one of Spain's finest white wines. Here are the top things you can do and places to visit while exploring this beautiful wine region:

Bodega Pazo de Señorans

- **Description**: A family-run winery known for its exceptional Albariño. Enjoy guided tours of the vineyard and tastings of their signature wines.
- **Location**: Finca Pazo de Señorans, 36637, Meis, Pontevedra.
- **How to Get There**: Accessible by car, about 30 minutes from Sanxenxo.
- **Opening Hours**: Monday to Saturday, 10:00 AM – 6:00 PM; closed on Sundays.
- **Entry Fee**: €12 for the guided tour and tasting.
- **Website**: www.pazodesenorans.com
- **Contact**: info@pazodesenorans.com.

Bodega Martin Códax

- **Description**: One of the most famous Albariño producers, offering comprehensive tours that include vineyard visits and wine tastings.
- **Location**: Rúa do Centeal, 22, 36630, Cambados, Pontevedra.

- **How to Get There**: Located in Cambados; reachable by car or local bus from Sanxenxo.
- **Opening Hours**: Monday to Friday, 10:00 AM – 6:00 PM; Saturday by appointment.
- **Entry Fee**: €15 for the guided tour and tasting.
- **Website**: www.martincodax.com
- **Contact**: info@martincodax.com.

Albariño Wine Route

- **Description**: A scenic route through the Rías Baixas, featuring various vineyards and charming villages. Perfect for wine lovers and those looking to explore the countryside.
- **Location**: Rías Baixas region, various stops along the route.
- **How to Get There**: Start in Cambados or Sanxenxo and follow the route by car or bike.
- **Opening Hours**: Open year-round.
- **Entry Fee**: Free to explore; tasting fees at individual wineries apply.

Enjoy your visit to the Albariño Wine Vineyards, where you can indulge in exquisite wines and breathtaking landscapes!

Combarro

Traditional Fishing Village with Historic Charm

Combarro is a picturesque fishing village known for its traditional architecture and stunning waterfront views. Here are the top things to do while you're there:

Visit the Hórreos

- **Description**: Explore the iconic stone granaries (hórreos) that dot the waterfront, showcasing Galician architectural heritage.
- **Location**: Rúa do Mar, Combarro.
- **How to Get There**: Easily accessible by foot from the village center.
- **Entry Fee**: Free.

Stroll Along the Seafront Promenade

- **Description**: Enjoy scenic views of the estuary and the charming traditional houses that line the waterfront.
- **Location**: Seafront area, Combarro.
- **How to Get There**: Walkable from anywhere in the village.
- **Entry Fee**: Free.

Visit the Church of San Francisco

- **Description**: A quaint church with beautiful architecture and a peaceful atmosphere.
- **Location**: Rúa do Porto, Combarro.
- **How to Get There**: Short walk from the hórreos.
- **Opening Hours**: Varies; generally open during daylight hours.
- **Entry Fee**: Free.

Enjoy your visit to Combarro, where history and beauty come together!

Asturias

Asturias is a stunning region in Northern Spain, known for its breathtaking landscapes, rich history, and unique culture. Nestled between the mountains and the Atlantic coast, it offers a variety of attractions, from charming medieval towns like **Oviedo** and **Gijón** to the spectacular natural beauty of the **Picos de Europa** National Park. You can enjoy outdoor adventures such as hiking, surfing, and exploring picturesque beaches. Don't miss the opportunity to savor traditional Asturian cuisine, including the famous **fabada** and local cider. Asturias promises an unforgettable experience for every traveler seeking nature and culture.

Oviedo

Medieval History and Culture

Oviedo Cathedral

Gothic Masterpiece with the Chapel of San Salvador

The **Oviedo Cathedral** is a must-visit landmark in Oviedo, showcasing stunning Gothic architecture. Here are the top things to do while you're there:

Explore the Cathedral Interior

- **Description**: Discover intricate chapels, beautiful stained glass, and the revered **Chapel of San Salvador**, housing sacred relics.
- **Location**: Plaza de Alfonso II, Oviedo.
- **How to Get There**: Centrally located; easily accessible on foot.
- **Opening Hours**: Daily from 10:00 AM to 8:00 PM.
- **Entry Fee**: Free; donations appreciated.

Visit the Cathedral Museum

- **Description**: Learn about the cathedral's history and art through fascinating exhibits.
- **Location**: Adjacent to the cathedral.

- **How to Get There**: Follow signs from the cathedral entrance.
- **Opening Hours**: 10:00 AM – 6:00 PM, closed Mondays.
- **Entry Fee**: €3.

Enjoy your visit to Oviedo Cathedral, a blend of history, spirituality, and architectural beauty!

San Julián de los Prados

Pre-Romanesque Church and UNESCO Site

San Julián de los Prados is a stunning example of pre-Romanesque architecture and a UNESCO World Heritage Site. Here are the top things to do during your visit:

Explore the Church's Interior

- **Description**: Marvel at the intricate frescoes and unique architecture that date back to the 9th century. The church is dedicated to Saint Julian and is one of the best-preserved examples of its kind.

- **Location**: Calle de San Julián, s/n, 33011 Oviedo.
- **How to Get There**: A short walk from the city center or accessible by bus.
- **Opening Hours**: Monday to Saturday from 10:00 AM to 1:00 PM and 5:00 PM to 8:00 PM; closed Sundays.
- **Entry Fee**: Free.

Visit the Cloister

- **Description**: The adjoining cloister offers a peaceful atmosphere and beautiful views of the church's architecture.
- **Location**: Adjacent to the church.
- **How to Get There**: Enter through the church entrance.
- **Opening Hours**: Same as the church.
- **Entry Fee**: Free.

Enjoy your visit to San Julián de los Prados, where history and beauty intertwine!

Plaza del Fontán

Historic Market Square and Meeting Point

Plaza del Fontán is a vibrant and historic market square in Oviedo, perfect for soaking in the local culture. Here are the top things to do during your visit:

Explore the Market Stalls

- **Description**: Visit the lively market held on Saturdays, featuring fresh produce, local cheeses, and handmade crafts. It's a great spot to buy souvenirs and taste local flavors.
- **Location**: Plaza del Fontán, Oviedo.
- **How to Get There**: Easily accessible on foot from the city center.
- **Opening Hours**: Market stalls operate on Saturdays from 9:00 AM to 2:00 PM.
- **Entry Fee**: Free.

Enjoy Local Cafés and Restaurants

- **Description**: Relax at one of the many outdoor cafés and sample traditional Asturian dishes like **fabada** or local cider.
- **Location**: Surrounding the square.
- **How to Get There**: Right off the square.
- **Opening Hours**: Varies by the establishment; typically from 10:00 AM onwards.
- **Entry Fee**: Free to enter; dining costs vary.

Admire the Architecture

- **Description**: Take in the beautiful 18th-century buildings and charming architecture that surround the square.
- **Location**: Throughout Plaza del Fontán.
- **Entry Fee**: Free.

Enjoy your time at Plaza del Fontán, where history and local culture come alive!

Gijón

Beaches, Parks, and Festivals

Playa de San Lorenzo

Gijón's Central Beach and Boardwalk

Playa de San Lorenzo is Gijón's most famous beach, offering a vibrant atmosphere and stunning coastal views. Here are the top things to do during your visit:

Relax on the Beach

- **Description**: Enjoy sunbathing or swimming in the clear waters of this popular urban beach, ideal for families and sun-seekers.
- **Location**: Playa de San Lorenzo, Gijón.
- **How to Get There**: Easily accessible by foot from the city center or via local buses (Lines 1 and 6).
- **Opening Hours**: Open 24/7.
- **Entry Fee**: Free.

Stroll the Promenade

- **Description**: Walk along the picturesque promenade lined with cafés, restaurants, and shops, perfect for people-watching.
- **Location**: Along the beach.
- **How to Get There**: Direct access from the beach.
- **Opening Hours**: Open 24/7.
- **Entry Fee**: Free.

Surfing and Water Sports

- **Description**: Try your hand at surfing or renting paddleboards and kayaks from local vendors.
- **Location**: Beachfront area.
- **How to Get There**: Head to the beach for rental kiosks.
- **Opening Hours**: Typically from 10:00 AM to 7:00 PM during the summer.
- **Entry Fee**: Prices vary by activity.

Enjoy your time at Playa de San Lorenzo, where sun and surf await!

Laboral Ciudad de la Cultura

Cultural Center with Art and Performances

Laboral Ciudad de la Cultura is a vibrant cultural hub in Gijón, offering a wide range of artistic experiences. Here are the top things to do during your visit:

Explore the Main Building

- **Description**: Discover the impressive architecture of this former school for arts, now housing galleries, theaters, and exhibition spaces.
- **Location**: Calle de los Caballeros, 13, 33203 Gijón.
- **How to Get There**: Accessible by bus (Lines 1 and 6) or a short walk from the city center.
- **Opening Hours**: Monday to Friday from 10:00 AM to 8:00 PM; weekends from 11:00 AM to 8:00 PM.

- **Entry Fee**: Free for general access; some exhibitions may have a fee.

Visit the Art Galleries

- **Description**: Enjoy rotating contemporary art exhibitions showcasing local and international artists.
- **Opening Hours**: Same as above.

Immerse yourself in the artistic spirit of Laboral Ciudad de la Cultura, where creativity flourishes!

Jardín Botánico Atlántico

Atlantic Botanic Gardens

The **Jardín Botánico Atlántico** in Gijón is a stunning botanical garden that showcases diverse plant species from the Atlantic region. Here are the top things to do during your visit:

Explore Themed Gardens

- **Description**: Wander through beautifully designed themed gardens, including the Mediterranean, wetland, and forest areas, each highlighting unique flora.
- **Location**: Calle de los Jardines, s/n, 33394 Gijón.
- **How to Get There**: Accessible by bus (Line 9) or a short taxi ride from the city center.
- **Opening Hours**: Daily from 10:00 AM to 7:00 PM (April to September); 10:00 AM to 5:00 PM (October to March).
- **Entry Fee**: €5 for adults; free for children under 12.

Relax in the Café

- **Description**: Enjoy a break at the garden café, offering refreshments with views of the beautiful surroundings.

Visit Jardín Botánico Atlántico for a serene escape into nature!

Picos de Europa

Nature's Masterpiece

Lagos de Covadonga

Stunning Mountain Lakes and Hiking Trails

Lagos de Covadonga is a breathtaking natural wonder in the **Picos de Europa** National Park, featuring picturesque lakes and stunning hiking trails. Here are the top things to do during your visit:

Visit the Lakes

- **Description**: Explore **Lago Enol** and **Lago Ercina**, two stunning glacial lakes surrounded by majestic mountains, perfect for picnicking and photography.
- **Location**: Lagos de Covadonga, Cangas de Onís, Asturias.

- **How to Get There**: Accessible by car or bus from Cangas de Onís. Note that access may require a fee during peak seasons.
- **Entry Fee**: Parking fee of around €5 during the summer months.

Hiking Trails

- **Description**: Enjoy numerous hiking trails with varying difficulty levels, offering breathtaking views and opportunities to see local wildlife.
- **Opening Hours**: Open year-round; trails accessible from dawn to dusk.

Visit the Covadonga Sanctuary

- **Description**: Explore the nearby **Basilica de Santa María la Real de Covadonga**, an impressive church with historical significance.
- **Contact**: +34 985 84 60 96.

Immerse yourself in the natural beauty of Lagos de Covadonga, where adventure awaits!

Cares Gorge Trail

Iconic Hiking Route Through the Mountains

The **Cares Gorge Trail** is one of the most breathtaking hiking routes in the **Picos de Europa**, offering stunning views of rugged cliffs and the crystal-clear Cares River. Here are the top things to do while exploring this iconic trail:

Hike the Trail

- **Description**: The approximately 12-kilometer path runs between **Poncebos** and **Cangas de Onís**, showcasing spectacular landscapes. It's suitable for all levels of hikers, with well-marked routes.
- **Location**: Start at **Poncebos** (Asturias) or **Cangas de Onís** (both accessible by car).
- **How to Get There**: Reach Poncebos via car or local bus.

- **Entry Fee**: Free.

Enjoy Scenic Views

- **Description**: Stop at various viewpoints along the trail to capture breathtaking photographs of the gorge and surrounding mountains.
- **Opening Hours**: Open year-round; best hiked during daylight hours.

Visit the Cares River

- **Description**: Take breaks by the river, enjoying the serene atmosphere and the sound of flowing water.

Get ready for an unforgettable adventure on the Cares Gorge Trail!

Sanctuary of Covadonga

Religious and Natural Site with Scenic Views

The **Sanctuary of Covadonga** is a stunning blend of spiritual significance and natural beauty, nestled in the heart of the **Picos de Europa**. Here are the top things to do during your visit:

Visit the Basilica of Santa María la Real de Covadonga

- **Description**: This majestic basilica, built in the early 20th century, features striking Romanesque architecture and is a pilgrimage site for many.
- **Location**: Covadonga, Cangas de Onís, Asturias.
- **How to Get There**: Accessible by car or bus from Cangas de Onís.
- **Opening Hours**: Daily from 9:00 AM to 8:00 PM.
- **Entry Fee**: Free.

Explore the Covadonga Caves

- **Description**: Discover the beautiful caves that house the shrine of **Sanctuary of Covadonga**, with impressive rock formations and historical significance.

- **Opening Hours**: 10:00 AM – 6:00 PM.
- **Entry Fee**: Free.

Enjoy Scenic Views

- **Description**: Take in breathtaking views of the surrounding mountains and lakes, perfect for photography and relaxation.

Visit the Sanctuary of Covadonga for a unique experience of faith and nature!

Cantabria

Cantabria is a captivating region in northern Spain, renowned for its stunning landscapes, rich history, and vibrant culture. Nestled between the mountains and the Atlantic Ocean, Cantabria boasts beautiful beaches like **Playa de Santander** and dramatic cliffs along the **Costa Cantabria**. The region is home to the **Altamira**

Caves, famous for their prehistoric rock art, and the charming medieval town of **Santillana del Mar**. Outdoor enthusiasts will love exploring the **Picos de Europa National Park**, offering incredible hiking trails and breathtaking views. Cantabria's culinary scene features fresh seafood and traditional dishes, making it a paradise for food lovers. With its blend of natural beauty, historical sites, and welcoming atmosphere, Cantabria promises an unforgettable experience for every traveler.

Santander

Elegant Seaside Escape

Palacio de la Magdalena

Royal Palace with Coastal Views

The **Palacio de la Magdalena** is a stunning seaside palace in Santander, offering a blend of history and breathtaking views. Here are the top things to do during your visit:

Tour the Palace

- **Description**: Explore the grand rooms and beautiful architecture of this former summer residence for the Spanish royal family.
- **Location**: Avenida de la Reina Victoria, s/n, 39005 Santander.
- **How to Get There**: Accessible by bus (Line 3) or a short walk from the city center.
- **Opening Hours**: Varies by season; typically from 10:00 AM to 6:00 PM.
- **Entry Fee**: Free; guided tours may have a fee.

Stroll the Gardens

- **Description**: Enjoy the beautifully landscaped gardens surrounding the palace, perfect for a relaxing walk.
- **Opening Hours**: Open 24/7.
- **Entry Fee**: Free.

Attend Events and Exhibitions

- **Description**: Check the schedule for cultural events, exhibitions, and concerts held throughout the year.
- **Website**: www.santander.es

Visit Palacio de la Magdalena for a perfect blend of history and stunning coastal scenery!

El Sardinero Beach

Elegant Beach with Gardens and Promenades

El Sardinero Beach is one of Santander's most picturesque spots, perfect for sunbathing and enjoying the coastal scenery. Here are the top things to do while visiting this beautiful beach:

Relax on the Beach

- **Description**: Soak up the sun on the expansive sandy shores, ideal for families and beach lovers.

- **Location**: Avenida de los Raqueros, 39005 Santander.
- **How to Get There**: Easily accessible by bus (Lines 1 and 3) or a short walk from the city center.
- **Opening Hours**: Open 24/7.
- **Entry Fee**: Free.

Stroll Along the Promenade

- **Description**: Enjoy a leisurely walk along the promenade, lined with palm trees and cafes, perfect for people-watching.
- **Opening Hours**: Open 24/7.
- **Entry Fee**: Free.

Visit the Jardines de Piquío

- **Description**: Explore the beautiful gardens that offer stunning views of the beach and the bay.
- **Location**: Adjacent to El Sardinero Beach.
- **Entry Fee**: Free.

El Sardinero Beach is the perfect place to unwind and enjoy the beauty of Santander!

Centro Botín

Modern Art Museum and Cultural Hub

Centro Botín is a stunning modern art museum in Santander, dedicated to contemporary art and culture. Below are the top things to do during your visit:

Explore the Art Exhibitions

- **Description**: Discover rotating exhibitions featuring works from renowned national and international artists, showcasing contemporary art in various forms.
- **Location**: Muelle de las Artes, s/n, 39002 Santander.
- **How to Get There**: Accessible by bus (Lines 1 and 3) or a short walk from the city center.

- **Opening Hours**: Tuesday to Sunday from 10:00 AM to 8:00 PM; closed Mondays.
- **Entry Fee**: €8 for adults; discounts available.

Visit the Roof Terrace

- **Description**: Enjoy breathtaking views of the bay and city from the rooftop terrace, a perfect spot for photos.
- **Opening Hours**: Same as the museum.
- **Entry Fee**: Free with museum entry.

Attend Cultural Events

- **Description**: Check the calendar for concerts, workshops, and lectures held throughout the year.
- **Website**: www.centrobotin.org

Immerse yourself in art and culture at Centro Botín!

Comillas and Santillana del Mar

Quaint Villages

Capricho de Gaudí

A Gaudí-Designed Architectural Gem

Capricho de Gaudí is a stunning example of the architect's unique style, located in the charming town of **Comillas**. Here are the top things to do during your visit:

Tour the Building

- **Description**: Explore this whimsical mansion, known for its colorful tiles, intricate ironwork, and fantastical design elements. It reflects Gaudí's distinctive approach to architecture.
- **Location**: Avenida de Gaudí, 1, 39520 Comillas, Cantabria.
- **How to Get There**: Easily reachable by car or bus from nearby towns.
- **Opening Hours**: Daily from 10:00 AM to 6:00 PM (April to October); 10:00 AM to 5:00 PM (November to March).

- **Entry Fee**: €5 for adults; discounts for children and seniors.

Explore the Gardens

- **Description**: Stroll through the beautifully landscaped gardens surrounding the mansion, offering great views and photo opportunities.
- **Entry Fee**: Free with museum ticket.

Discover the magic of Capricho de Gaudí, where architecture meets fantasy!

Altamira Caves

Prehistoric Cave Paintings and Visitor Center

The **Altamira Caves** are a UNESCO World Heritage Site famous for their stunning prehistoric cave paintings. Here are the top things to do during your visit:

Explore the Caves

- **Description**: Marvel at the intricate cave paintings, estimated to be over 36,000 years old, showcasing bison and other animals. Access to the original cave is restricted, but replicas are available.
- **Location**: Cueva de Altamira, 39330 Santillana del Mar, Cantabria.
- **How to Get There**: Reachable by car; parking available nearby.
- **Opening Hours**: Daily from 9:30 AM to 7:30 PM (April to September); 9:30 AM to 5:00 PM (October to March).
- **Entry Fee**: €3 for adults; free for children under 18.

Visit the Visitor Center

- **Description**: Learn about the significance of the paintings and the history of the caves through informative exhibits.
- **Opening Hours**: Same as above.
- **Entry Fee**: Included with cave entry.

Explore the Surrounding Park

- **Description**: Enjoy walking trails in the natural park surrounding the caves, perfect for a scenic hike.

Discover the wonder of Altamira Caves, where history comes alive!

Santillana del Mar

Charming Medieval Village with Historic Streets

Santillana del Mar is a picturesque medieval village, renowned for its cobbled streets and rich history. Here are the top things to do during your visit:

Visit the Colegiata de Santa Juliana

- **Description**: This stunning Romanesque church dates back to the 12th century and features beautiful stone carvings and an impressive façade.

- **Location**: Plaza de la Colegiata, 39330 Santillana del Mar.
- **How to Get There**: Accessible by car; parking is available nearby.
- **Opening Hours**: Daily from 10:00 AM to 1:00 PM and 4:00 PM to 7:00 PM.
- **Entry Fee**: Free.

Explore the Museo de la Tortura

- **Description**: Discover fascinating and macabre exhibits related to historical torture devices.
- **Location**: Rúa de la Cruz, 8, 39330 Santillana del Mar.
- **How to Get There**: A short walk from the main square.
- **Opening Hours**: 10:00 AM to 7:00 PM daily.
- **Entry Fee**: €5.

Stroll Through the Historic Streets

- **Description**: Wander the charming streets, lined with medieval houses, shops, and cafés, perfect for soaking in the village atmosphere.
- **Entry Fee**: Free.

Enjoy your visit to Santillana del Mar, a delightful step back in time!

Cabárceno Nature Park

Wildlife Experience

Cabárceno Natural Park

A Unique Wildlife Park with Free-Roaming Animals

Cabárceno Natural Park is a captivating wildlife park located in Cantabria, showcasing animals in a natural habitat. Here are the top things to do during your visit:

Observe Free-Roaming Animals

- **Description**: Explore the park's diverse wildlife, including elephants, lions, and native species, roaming freely in expansive enclosures.
- **Location**: Cabárceno, 39600, Cantabria.
- **How to Get There**: Accessible by car, about 20 minutes from Santander; follow signs from the A67 highway.
- **Opening Hours**: Daily from 10:00 AM to 7:00 PM (April to September); 10:00 AM to 5:00 PM (October to March).
- **Entry Fee**: €30 for adults; discounts for children and seniors.

Visit the Education Center

- **Description**: Learn about wildlife conservation and local flora through engaging exhibits and activities.
- **Opening Hours**: Same as the park.
- **Entry Fee**: Included with park entry.

Enjoy Scenic Views

- **Description**: Take advantage of the park's stunning landscapes and viewpoints, ideal for photography.

Experience the wonders of nature at Cabárceno Natural Park!

Elephant and Lion Exhibits

Top Wildlife Experiences at Cabárceno Natural Park

At **Cabárceno Natural Park**, the **Elephant and Lion Exhibits** are must-see attractions for wildlife enthusiasts. Here's what to expect during your visit:

Elephant Exhibit

- **Description**: Watch majestic Asian elephants roam freely in a spacious, natural habitat. The park provides opportunities to see their social behaviors and feeding routines.
- **Location**: Inside Cabárceno Natural Park.

- **How to Get There**: Accessible via park pathways; follow signs from the entrance.
- **Opening Hours**: Daily from 10:00 AM to 7:00 PM (April to September); 10:00 AM to 5:00 PM (October to March).
- **Entry Fee**: Included with park admission.

Lion Exhibit

- **Description**: Observe a pride of African lions in a well-designed enclosure that mimics their natural environment, offering a thrilling viewing experience.
- **Location**: Within Cabárceno Natural Park.
- **Entry Fee**: Included with park admission.

Explore these incredible exhibits and witness wildlife up close at Cabárceno!

Aerial Cable Car

Scenic Views of Cabárceno Natural Park

The **Aerial Cable Car** at **Cabárceno Natural Park** offers a breathtaking way to experience the stunning landscapes and wildlife from above. Here's what you need to know:

Enjoy Panoramic Views

- **Description**: The cable car ride provides stunning aerial views of the park's diverse habitats and free-roaming animals, making it a perfect opportunity for photography.
- **Location**: Cabárceno Natural Park, 39600, Cantabria.
- **How to Get There**: Accessible via park pathways; look for signage directing you to the cable car station.
- **Opening Hours**: Daily from 10:00 AM to 7:00 PM (April to September); 10:00 AM to 5:00 PM (October to March).
- **Entry Fee**: €8 for a round trip.

Relaxing Experience

- **Description**: The ride lasts about 15 minutes each way, allowing you to soak in the beauty of the park and its surroundings.

For an unforgettable view of nature, don't miss the Aerial Cable Car at Cabárceno!

Basque Country

Basque Country is a vibrant and culturally rich region in northern Spain, known for its unique language, breathtaking landscapes, and world-renowned cuisine. From the bustling streets of **Bilbao**, home to the iconic **Guggenheim Museum**, to the picturesque beaches of **San Sebastián**, this area offers a diverse range of experiences. Outdoor enthusiasts can explore the stunning **Picos de Europa** mountains, while food lovers can indulge in pintxos, the Basque version of tapas, in charming local taverns. With its rich history, colorful festivals, and strong traditions, the Basque

Country promises an unforgettable adventure for every traveler seeking culture, nature, and gastronomy.

Bilbao

Guggenheim Museum and Modern Architecture

Guggenheim Museum

Iconic Museum of Contemporary Art

The **Guggenheim Museum** in Bilbao is a stunning architectural marvel and a must-visit for art lovers. Here are the top things to do during your visit:

Explore the Permanent Collection

- **Description**: Discover an impressive collection of modern and contemporary art, featuring works by renowned artists such as Jeff Koons, Richard Serra, and Anish Kapoor.

- **Location**: Abandoibarra Etorbidea, 2, 48001 Bilbao.
- **How to Get There**: Easily accessible by tram (Bilbao Tram) or bus (Line 77).
- **Opening Hours**: Tuesday to Sunday from 10:00 AM to 8:00 PM; closed Mondays.
- **Entry Fee**: €16 for adults; discounts for students and seniors.

Visit Temporary Exhibitions

- **Description**: Check out rotating exhibitions that showcase contemporary works and installations from around the world.
- **Entry Fee**: Included with general admission.

Enjoy the Surrounding Sculpture Garden

- **Description**: Stroll through the outdoor space featuring impressive sculptures, including the famous **Puppy** by Jeff Koons.
- **Entry Fee**: Free.

Experience the beauty and creativity at the Guggenheim Museum, a highlight of Bilbao!

Zubizuri Bridge

Modern Pedestrian Bridge Designed by Santiago Calatrava

The **Zubizuri Bridge**, also known as the "White Bridge," is a stunning architectural landmark in Bilbao, designed by renowned architect Santiago Calatrava. Here are the top things to do during your visit:

Walk Across the Bridge

- **Description**: Enjoy a leisurely stroll across this iconic pedestrian bridge, featuring a unique curved design and panoramic views of the city.
- **Location**: Campo de Volantín, s/n, 48007 Bilbao.

- **How to Get There**: Easily accessible from the city center; walkable from the **Guggenheim Museum**.
- **Opening Hours**: Open 24/7.
- **Entry Fee**: Free.

Photograph the Architecture

- **Description**: Capture stunning photos of the bridge's modern design, especially at sunset when it's beautifully lit.
- **Entry Fee**: Free.

Explore Surrounding Areas

- **Description**: Discover nearby parks and pathways along the **Nervión River**, perfect for a scenic walk or bike ride.

Visit the Zubizuri Bridge for a blend of art, architecture, and stunning views of Bilbao!

Casco Viejo

Bilbao's Old Town with Historic Streets and Pintxos Bars

Casco Viejo is the charming Old Town of Bilbao, filled with narrow streets, historic buildings, and vibrant culture. Here are the top things to do during your visit:

Explore Plaza Nueva

- **Description**: This beautiful square is surrounded by neoclassical buildings and is the perfect spot to enjoy pintxos at outdoor cafés.
- **Location**: Plaza Nueva, 48005 Bilbao.
- **How to Get There**: Easily accessible by tram (Bilbao Tram) or on foot from the city center.
- **Opening Hours**: Open 24/7; cafés typically open from 10:00 AM.
- **Entry Fee**: Free.

Visit the Mercado de la Ribera

- **Description**: Discover one of the largest markets in Europe, offering fresh produce, local delicacies, and artisanal products.
- **Location**: Calle de la Ribera, 1, 48005 Bilbao.
- **How to Get There**: A short walk from Plaza Nueva.
- **Opening Hours**: Daily from 8:00 AM to 10:00 PM.
- **Entry Fee**: Free.

Enjoy Pintxos Bars

- **Description**: Sample traditional Basque cuisine at local pintxos bars, where small plates are served with drinks.
- **Location**: Throughout Casco Viejo.
- **Entry Fee**: Free to enter; cost varies per dish.

Immerse yourself in the history and flavors of Casco Viejo for an unforgettable experience!

San Sebastián

Culinary Capital and La Concha Beach

La Concha Beach

One of Europe's Best Urban Beaches

La Concha Beach in San Sebastián is celebrated for its picturesque bay, golden sands, and vibrant atmosphere. Here are the top things to do during your visit:

Relax on the Beach

- **Description**: Enjoy sunbathing and swimming in the calm waters of this beautiful urban beach, ideal for families and sun-seekers.
- **Location**: La Concha, 20007 San Sebastián.
- **How to Get There**: Easily accessible by bus (Line 26) or on foot from the city center.
- **Opening Hours**: Open 24/7.
- **Entry Fee**: Free.

Stroll the Promenade

- **Description**: Take a leisurely walk along the scenic promenade, lined with palm trees, cafés, and shops, perfect for people-watching.
- **Entry Fee**: Free.

Rent Water Sports Equipment

- **Description**: Try kayaking or paddleboarding with equipment rentals available along the beach.
- **How to Get There**: Rental kiosks located on the beach.
- **Opening Hours**: Varies by season; generally from 10:00 AM to 7:00 PM.
- **Entry Fee**: Prices vary by activity.

Experience the beauty and energy of La Concha Beach for an unforgettable day by the sea!

Monte Igueldo Funicular

Scenic Rides with Panoramic Views of the City

The **Monte Igueldo Funicular** offers a breathtaking journey to the summit of Monte Igueldo, providing stunning views of San Sebastián and the surrounding coastline. Here are the top things to do during your visit:

Ride the Funicular

- **Description**: Enjoy a scenic ride up the funicular railway, which ascends at a steep incline, showcasing spectacular vistas along the way.
- **Location**: Paseo del Funicular, 1, 20008 San Sebastián.
- **How to Get There**: Accessible by bus (Line 16) from the city center or by walking to the base station.
- **Opening Hours**: Daily from 10:00 AM to 8:00 PM (April to October); 10:00 AM to 6:00 PM (November to March).
- **Entry Fee**: €3.20 for a round trip.

Visit the Amusement Park

- **Description**: At the top, enjoy a vintage amusement park with rides and attractions, perfect for families.
- **Entry Fee**: Free; individual rides may have fees.

Enjoy Scenic Lookouts

- **Description**: Take in panoramic views of the city, bay, and mountains from the viewing platforms.
- **Entry Fee**: Free.

Experience the beauty of San Sebastián from above at Monte Igueldo Funicular!

Parte Vieja

Old Town with World-Famous Pintxo Bars

Parte Vieja is San Sebastián's bustling Old Town, renowned for its vibrant atmosphere and delicious pintxo bars. Here are the top things to do:

Sample Pintxos

- **Description**: Indulge in local specialties at numerous pintxo bars, where you can enjoy small dishes and local wines.
- **Location**: Calle 31 de Agosto, 20003 San Sebastián.
- **How to Get There**: Easily accessible on foot from the city center.
- **Opening Hours**: Typically from 11:00 AM to 11:00 PM.
- **Entry Fee**: Free to enter; prices vary by pintxo.

Visit Plaza de la Constitución

- **Description**: Admire the beautiful square surrounded by historic buildings and lively cafés.
- **Entry Fee**: Free.

Enjoy the culinary delights and rich culture of Parte Vieja!

Vitoria-Gasteiz

Spain's Green Capital

Cathedral of Santa María

A Gothic Cathedral in the Heart of the City

The **Cathedral of Santa María** is a stunning example of Gothic architecture in Vitoria-Gasteiz. Here's what to do during your visit:

Explore the Cathedral Interior

- **Description**: Discover beautiful stained glass, intricate carvings, and the serene atmosphere within the cathedral.
- **Location**: Plaza de la Virgen Blanca, 01001 Vitoria-Gasteiz.

- **How to Get There**: Accessible by foot from the city center; near major bus routes.
- **Opening Hours**: Monday to Saturday from 10:00 AM to 6:00 PM; Sundays from 12:00 PM to 2:00 PM.
- **Entry Fee**: €5 for adults; discounts for students and seniors.

Attend a Guided Tour

- **Description**: Join a guided tour to learn about the cathedral's history and architecture.
- **Website**: www.vitoria-gasteiz.org

Experience the beauty and history of the Cathedral of Santa María!

Green Ring

Urban Park Network Encircling the City

The **Green Ring** is a picturesque network of parks and pathways encircling Vitoria-Gasteiz, perfect for outdoor activities. Here's what to do during your visit:

Enjoy Walking and Biking Trails

- **Description**: Explore over 30 kilometers of trails ideal for walking, jogging, and cycling, offering scenic views of nature and the city.
- **Location**: Various access points around the city.
- **How to Get There**: Easily accessible from multiple neighborhoods; follow signs for the Green Ring.
- **Opening Hours**: Open 24/7.
- **Entry Fee**: Free.

Visit Parque de la Florida

- **Description**: A beautiful park featuring lush gardens, fountains, and a playground.
- **Entry Fee**: Free.

Discover the natural beauty of Vitoria-Gasteiz at the Green Ring!

Plaza de la Virgen Blanca

Historic Square and Lively Hub

Plaza de la Virgen Blanca is a vibrant square in Vitoria-Gasteiz, known for its historic significance and lively atmosphere. Here's what to do during your visit:

Admire the Monument to the Virgen Blanca

- **Description**: View the iconic statue dedicated to the city's patron saint, surrounded by beautiful gardens.
- **Location**: Plaza de la Virgen Blanca, 01001 Vitoria-Gasteiz.
- **How to Get There**: Centrally located; easily reachable by foot or public transport.
- **Opening Hours**: Open 24/7.
- **Entry Fee**: Free.

Explore Nearby Cafés and Shops

- **Description**: Enjoy local cuisine and drinks at surrounding cafés, perfect for people-watching and soaking in the atmosphere.
- **Entry Fee**: Free to enter; dining costs vary.

Experience the charm and culture of Plaza de la Virgen Blanca!

Navarra

Navarra is a diverse and enchanting region in northern Spain, known for its rich history, stunning landscapes, and vibrant culture. From the historic city of **Pamplona**, famous for the thrilling **Running of the Bulls** during the San Fermín festival, to the picturesque valleys and lush forests of the **Baztan Valley**, Navarra offers something for every traveler. Outdoor enthusiasts can explore the breathtaking **Pyrenees mountains**, while history buffs will appreciate ancient sites like the **Castle of Javier** and charming medieval towns. Navarra is also celebrated for its exceptional cuisine, featuring delicious local dishes and excellent wines. With its unique blend of tradition and modernity, Navarra promises an unforgettable experience for all who visit.

Pamplona

Running of the Bulls and Historical Sights

Plaza del Castillo

Pamplona's Central Square with Cafés and Events

Plaza del Castillo is the heart of Pamplona, known for its lively atmosphere and historical significance. Here are the top things to do during your visit:

Relax at Outdoor Cafés

- **Description**: Enjoy a coffee or pintxos at one of the many cafés lining the square, perfect for people-watching.

- **Location**: Plaza del Castillo, 31001 Pamplona.
- **How to Get There**: Centrally located; easily accessible on foot.
- **Opening Hours**: Varies by establishment; generally from 8:00 AM to midnight.
- **Entry Fee**: Free to enter; dining costs vary.

Attend Local Events

- **Description**: Participate in various cultural events and festivals held throughout the year, including concerts and markets.
- **Entry Fee**: Free.

Experience the vibrant life of Pamplona at Plaza del Castillo!

Pamplona Cathedral

Stunning Gothic Cathedral and Cloister

The **Pamplona Cathedral** is a remarkable Gothic structure that showcases stunning architecture and rich history. Here's what to do during your visit:

Explore the Cathedral Interior

- **Description**: Admire the impressive altarpiece, beautiful stained glass, and intricate chapels within the cathedral.
- **Location**: Calle Dormitalería, 1, 31001 Pamplona.
- **How to Get There**: Centrally located; easily reachable on foot from the city center.
- **Opening Hours**: Monday to Saturday from 10:00 AM to 6:00 PM; Sunday from 12:00 PM to 1:00 PM.
- **Entry Fee**: €3 for adults; free for children under 12.

Visit the Cloister

- **Description**: Discover the serene cloister, featuring beautiful arches and a peaceful atmosphere.
- **Entry Fee**: Included with cathedral admission.

Experience the beauty and history of Pamplona Cathedral!

San Fermín Festival

World-Famous Running of the Bulls Event

The **San Fermín Festival** in Pamplona is a vibrant celebration renowned for its iconic **Running of the Bulls**, attracting thousands each July. Here's what to experience:

Attend the Running of the Bulls

1. **Description**: Experience the thrilling morning event where runners chase bulls through the streets to the bullring.

2. **Location**: Various streets in Pamplona, beginning at Calle Santo Domingo.
3. **How to Get There**: Easily accessible by foot from the city center.
4. **Event Dates**: July 6-14 annually.
5. **Entry Fee**: Free to watch; early arrival is recommended for the best views.

Join Festivities and Parades

6. **Description**: Enjoy daily parades, traditional music, and cultural events throughout the festival.
7. **Entry Fee**: Free.

Immerse yourself in the excitement of the San Fermín Festival, a unique cultural experience!

Baztan Valley

Hidden Villages and Verdant Scenery

Elizondo

Traditional Village with Picturesque Streets

Elizondo is a charming village in the Baztan Valley, known for its traditional Basque architecture and stunning landscapes. Here's what to explore during your visit:

Wander the Streets

- **Description**: Stroll through the picturesque streets lined with historic buildings, colorful facades, and beautiful balconies.
- **Location**: Elizondo, 31700 Baztan, Navarra.
- **How to Get There**: Accessible by car or bus from Pamplona (approximately 45 minutes).
- **Opening Hours**: Open 24/7.
- **Entry Fee**: Free.

Visit the Church of Santiago

- **Description**: Explore this charming 18th-century church featuring beautiful interior artwork.
- **Location**: Plaza de la Iglesia, Elizondo.

- **Opening Hours**: Typically open during daylight hours.
- **Entry Fee**: Free.

Discover the serene beauty and rich culture of Elizondo!

Urdax Caves

Natural Cave Formations with Guided Tours

The **Urdax Caves** are a fascinating natural wonder located in the Baztan Valley, showcasing impressive rock formations and ancient stalactites. Here's what to do during your visit:

Take a Guided Tour

- **Description**: Explore the stunning cave system with a knowledgeable guide who will share insights about its geology and history.
- **Location**: Urdax, Navarra.

- **How to Get There**: Accessible by car, approximately 30 minutes from Elizondo.
- **Opening Hours**: Daily from 10:00 AM to 5:00 PM (April to October); hours may vary in winter.
- **Entry Fee**: €8 for adults; discounts for children and seniors.

Discover the Surrounding Nature

- **Description**: Enjoy hiking trails in the beautiful surrounding landscape, perfect for outdoor enthusiasts.
- **Entry Fee**: Free.

Experience the beauty and mystery of the Urdax Caves!

Bertiz Natural Park

A Serene Park with Botanical Gardens

Bertiz Natural Park is a tranquil oasis in Navarra, featuring lush landscapes and diverse plant life. Here's what to do during your visit:

Explore the Botanical Gardens

- **Description**: Discover a variety of native and exotic plants in beautifully landscaped gardens, perfect for nature lovers and families.
- **Location**: Bertiz Natural Park, 31796, Navarra.
- **How to Get There**: Accessible by car; located about 30 minutes from Elizondo.
- **Opening Hours**: Daily from 9:00 AM to 6:00 PM (April to October); reduced hours in winter.
- **Entry Fee**: Free for the park; specific areas may have fees.

Hiking Trails

- **Description**: Enjoy scenic walking trails through the park, ideal for hiking and birdwatching.
- **Entry Fee**: Free.

Immerse yourself in the natural beauty of Bertiz Natural Park!

Chapter 5

Where to Stay

Luxury Hotels in Northern Spain

Hotel Maria Cristina, San Sebastián

- **Address:** República Argentina K., 4, 20004 Donostia, Gipuzkoa, Spain
- **Price Range:** €250 - €450 per night
- **Features and Amenities:** Luxurious rooms, spa services, fine dining restaurant, free Wi-Fi, and fitness center.
- **Booking Platforms:** Booking.com, Expedia, official hotel website.
- **Local Regulations and Customs:** Check-in at 3:00 PM, check-out by noon. Tipping is appreciated but not mandatory.
- **Special Features:** Family-friendly with options for connecting rooms; pet-friendly.

- **Reviews**: Rated 9.5/10 on Booking.com; praised for its location and service.
- **Transportation**: Close to La Concha Beach and the city center; accessible via public transport and taxis.
- **Contact Information**: Front Desk: +34 943 43 76 00

Parador de Argómaniz

- **Address:** Ctra. N--1, km 363, 01192 Argómaniz, Álava, Spain
- **Price Range**: €120 - €200 per night
- **Features and Amenities**: Historical building, restaurant, garden, and outdoor pool.
- **Booking Platforms**: Paradores' official website, Booking.com.
- **Local Regulations and Customs**: Check-in at 2:00 PM, check-out by noon. Tipping is generally not expected.

- **Special Features**: Ideal for families and solo travelers; accessible for persons with disabilities.
- **Reviews**: Rated 8.8/10; guests love the peaceful surroundings and excellent dining.
- **Transportation**: About 10 km from Vitoria-Gasteiz; taxi services available; public transport options are limited.
- **Contact Information**: Front Desk: +34 945 29 32 00

Hotel Tres Reyes, Pamplona

- **Address:** C. Taconera, 1, 31001 Pamplona, Navarra, Spain
- **Price Range**: €100 - €180 per night
- **Features and Amenities**: Comfortable rooms, fitness center, free Wi-Fi, and on-site parking.
- **Booking Platforms**: Hotels.com, official hotel website.

- **Local Regulations and Customs**: Check-in at 2:00 PM, check-out by noon. Tipping is common in restaurants.
- **Special Features**: Family-friendly; offers wheelchair-accessible rooms.
- **Reviews**: Rated 8.6/10; noted for its helpful staff and location near the city center.
- **Transportation**: Close to major attractions; bus and taxi services readily available.
- **Contact Information**: Front Desk: +34 948 22 66 00

Hotel de Londres y de Inglaterra, San Sebastián

- **Address:** Zubieta Kalea, 2, 20007 Donostia, Gipuzkoa, Spain
- **Price Range**: €200 - €400 per night
- **Features and Amenities**: Beachfront views, restaurant, bar, and free Wi-Fi.
- **Booking Platforms**: Expedia, Booking.com, official hotel website.

- **Local Regulations and Customs**: Check-in at 3:00 PM, check-out by noon. Tipping is customary in restaurants.
- **Special Features**: Family-friendly; offers cribs and extra beds for children.
- **Reviews**: Rated 9.2/10; guests appreciate the beautiful views and central location.
- **Transportation**: Easily accessible by bus and taxi; walking distance to major attractions.
- **Contact Information**: Front Desk: +34 943 44 07 70

Albergue Plaza, Pamplona

- **Address:** C. Navarrería, 35, 31001 Pamplona, Navarra, Spain
- **Price Range**: €25 - €60 per night (dormitory and private rooms)

- **Features and Amenities**: Shared kitchen, common area, free Wi-Fi, and bike rental services.
- **Booking Platforms**: Hostelworld, Booking.com.
- **Local Regulations and Customs**: Check-in at 2:00 PM, check-out by 11:00 AM. Tipping is not expected but appreciated.
- **Special Features**: Great for solo travelers and backpackers; accessible for persons with disabilities.
- **Reviews**: Rated 9.0/10; praised for its cleanliness and friendly atmosphere.
- **Transportation**: Public transport and taxis are available close to the city center.
- **Contact Information**: Front Desk: +34 620 91 39 68

Rural Stays Accommodations and Casas Rurales

Casa Rural Ervitena

- **Address**: Calle San Juan, 10, 31195 Oteiza, Navarra, Spain
- **Price Range**: €80 - €150 per night
- **Features and Amenities**: Fully equipped kitchen, Free Wi-Fi, Garden and BBQ facilities, Flat-screen TV, Washing machine, Outdoor seating area
- **Local Regulations and Customs**:Check-in: 5:00 PM to 8:00 PM, Check-out: 10:00 AM to 12:00 PM
- **Special Features**: Family-friendly; suitable for pets upon request; wheelchair-accessible rooms available.
- **Reviews**: Rated 9.4/10; guests love the spaciousness, cleanliness, and welcoming atmosphere.

- **Transportation**: A car is recommended; local bus services are available to Pamplona (approximately 10 km away).
- **Contact Information**:
  - Front Desk: +34 948 52 25 43
  - Local Tourism Office: +34 948 42 62 10

Casa Rural Ervitena offers a delightful rural escape with all the comforts of home!

La Casa del Organista

- **Address**: C. de los Hornos, 4, 39330 Santillana del Mar, Cantabria, Spain
- **Price Range**: €100 - €200 per night
- **Features and Amenities**: Historic building, kitchen, free Wi-Fi, garden, and terrace.
- **Booking Platforms**: Booking.com, Expedia.
- **Local Regulations and Customs**: Check-in at 3:00 PM, check-out by noon. Tipping is appreciated.
- **Special Features**: Great for couples and solo travelers; pet-friendly.

- **Reviews**: Rated 9.4/10; praised for its unique charm and location.
- **Transportation**: Walkable from local attractions; nearby bus services available.
- **Contact Information**: +34 942 84 03 52

Casa Rural La Casa de las Flores

- **Address**: C. Chorrillo, 31, 45125 Pulgar, Toledo, Spain
- **Price Range**: €90 - €160 per night
- **Features and Amenities**: Garden, terrace, kitchen, and barbecue area.
- **Booking Platforms**: Airbnb, Booking.com.
- **Local Regulations and Customs**: Check-in at 4:00 PM, check-out by 11:00 AM. Tipping is customary.
- **Special Features**: Family-friendly with spacious rooms and outdoor play area.

- **Reviews**: Rated 9.2/10; visitors love the peaceful environment and beautiful gardens.
- **Transportation**: A car is recommended; local buses connect to nearby towns.
- **Contact Information**: +34 639 50 54 30

Casa Rural El Valle

- **Address**: Las Rosas la Cuesta, 29A, 38915 San Andrés, Spain
- **Price Range**: €80 - €140 per night
- **Features and Amenities**: Rustic decor, free Wi-Fi, garden, and picnic area.
- **Booking Platforms**: Booking.com, Ruralidays.
- **Local Regulations and Customs**: Check-in at 2:00 PM, check-out by 12:00 PM. Tipping is optional.
- **Special Features**: Accessible for persons with disabilities; suitable for nature lovers.
- **Reviews**: Rated 9.0/10; guests appreciate the serene location and hospitality.

- **Transportation**: Local bus service available; parking on-site.
- **Contact Information**: +34 943 77 78 90; Local Tourism Office: +34 943 10 52 62.

Casa Rural La Loma

- **Address**: Los Gancheros, 6, 16191 Nohales, España
- **Price Range**: €70 - €130 per night
- **Features and Amenities**: Free Wi-Fi, outdoor pool, garden, and shared kitchen.
- **Booking Platforms**: Airbnb, HomeAway.
- **Local Regulations and Customs**: Check-in at 3:00 PM, check-out by 11:00 AM. Tipping is appreciated but not required.
- **Special Features**: Ideal for families and pet owners; offers family rooms.
- **Reviews**: Rated 9.3/10; guests highlight the friendly service and scenic views.

- **Transportation**: Car recommended; local taxis available.

Tips for Booking Accommodation During Peak Season

Booking accommodation during peak season can be challenging, but with the right strategies, you can secure a great stay. Here are some tips:

1. **Book Early**: Popular destinations fill up quickly during peak season. Aim to book your accommodation at least 3-6 months in advance to secure the best options and prices.
2. **Be Flexible with Dates**: If possible, adjust your travel dates to avoid weekends or major holidays, when prices are higher and availability is limited.
3. **Use Multiple Platforms**: Compare prices across various booking platforms like Airbnb, Booking.com, and Expedia. Each may offer different deals or cancellation policies.

4. **Consider Alternative Locations**: Staying slightly outside the main tourist areas can often provide better rates and a more local experience.

5. **Read Reviews**: Check recent reviews to ensure the accommodation meets your expectations and is well-maintained.

By planning ahead and being flexible, you can enhance your travel experience even during the busiest times.

Chapter 6

Gastronomy and Culinary Experiences

Welcome to the vibrant world of gastronomy in Northern Spain! This region is a culinary treasure, renowned for its diverse flavors and rich traditions. From the famous pintxos of San Sebastián to the hearty dishes of the Basque Country and the exquisite wines of La Rioja, you'll find a feast for the senses at every turn. Don't miss the chance to explore local markets, dine in cozy taverns, and participate in cooking classes that immerse you in the art of Spanish cuisine. Whether you're a food enthusiast or simply looking to savor new experiences, Northern Spain promises unforgettable culinary adventures that will delight your palate and enrich your travels.

Must-Try Dishes in Northern Spain

When visiting Northern Spain, several must-try dishes showcase the region's rich culinary heritage:

Pintxos: These small snacks are typically served on skewers, featuring a variety of toppings such as cured meats, seafood, and vegetables. They burst with flavor and are best enjoyed in the lively bars of San Sebastián.

Bacalao al Pil-Pil: A Basque dish of cod cooked in olive oil, garlic, and chili, creating a rich, flavorful sauce. The fish is tender and flaky, perfectly complementing the sauce.

Fabada Asturiana: A hearty bean stew from Asturias made with faba beans, chorizo, and morcilla (blood sausage). It's rich, comforting, and ideal for chilly days.

Chuletón: A massive ribeye steak, often grilled over an open flame. It's juicy, tender, and typically served rare, showcasing the region's excellent beef.

Txakoli: A slightly sparkling, dry white wine from the Basque Country, known for its crisp acidity and citrus notes, perfect for pairing with seafood.

Cider (Sidra): A traditional Asturian beverage, this fermented apple cider is slightly sour and served from a height to aerate it, enhancing its flavors.

Marmitako: A delicious tuna and potato stew from the Cantabrian coast, seasoned with peppers and onions, offering a taste of the sea.

Bollos Preñados: Savory buns stuffed with chorizo or other meats, popular as street food, offering a satisfying snack on the go.

Tarta de Santiago: An almond cake from Galicia, flavored with lemon and dusted with powdered sugar, perfect for dessert lovers.

Arroz con Leche: A creamy rice pudding made with milk, sugar, and cinnamon, providing a sweet end to any meal.

Exploring these dishes will give you a true taste of Northern Spain's rich culinary heritage!

Galician Seafood

When in Northern Spain, don't miss these five Galician seafood delights:

1. **Pulpo a la Gallega**: Tender octopus seasoned with paprika, sea salt, and olive oil, served on a wooden platter. Its smoky flavor and soft texture make it a must-try.

2. **Percebes (Goose Barnacles)**: These unique, shell-like creatures are harvested from rocky coastlines. Their briny, oceanic flavor is a delicacy, often enjoyed simply steamed with salt.

3. **Mejillones (Mussels)**: Galician mussels are large and juicy, often prepared in a variety of ways, including steamed with a tangy sauce of onions, tomatoes, and spices.

4. **Sardinas a la Plancha**: Grilled sardines, typically served with a sprinkle of sea salt. Their rich, oily flavor shines through when cooked over an open flame.

5. **Raxo**: A Galician specialty of marinated fried fish, often made with small pieces of cod or hake, served with potatoes and a side of spicy sauce.

These dishes showcase Galicia's rich seafood heritage and are essential for any culinary adventure!

Asturian Delights

Here are five Asturian delights you must try when visiting Northern Spain:

1. **Fabada Asturiana**: This hearty bean stew is the region's signature dish, made with large white beans, chorizo, morcilla (blood sausage), and pork. Rich and comforting, it's perfect for chilly days.

2. **Cider (Sidra)**: Asturian cider is a traditional drink, fermented from local apples. It's slightly sour and often served from a height to aerate it. Enjoy it alongside your meals for an authentic experience.

3. **Queso de Cabrales**: This blue cheese, made from cow's, goat's, or sheep's milk, is creamy with a sharp, tangy flavor. It's typically served with bread or as part of a cheese platter.

4. **Churros con Chocolate**: A beloved snack, these deep-fried dough pastries are crispy on the outside and soft inside, often served with a thick, rich chocolate dipping sauce.

5. **Arroz con Leche**: This creamy rice pudding is flavored with cinnamon and lemon zest, providing a sweet finish to any meal. It's a comforting dessert that reflects the region's culinary heritage.

These Asturian delights are a must for anyone looking to savor the flavors of Northern Spain!

Basque Cuisine

Here are five Basque dishes you must try when visiting Northern Spain:

1. **Pintxos**: These small snacks are a staple of Basque cuisine, typically served on skewers or bread. They come with a variety of toppings, such as marinated anchovies, peppers, and seafood, offering bold flavors in every bite.

2. **Bacalao a la Vizcaína**: This dish features salt cod cooked in a rich, spicy tomato sauce made with red peppers, onions, and garlic. The savory flavors of the sauce complement the tender fish perfectly.

3. **Txangurro**: A delicious spider crab dish, txangurro is usually served in its shell with a mixture of crab meat, onions, and spices. It's often enjoyed as a tapa or as part of a larger seafood feast.

4. **Marmitako**: This traditional tuna and potato stew is made with fresh fish, peppers, and onions,

simmered to create a hearty and flavorful dish. It's perfect for seafood lovers seeking comfort food.

5. **Gâteau Basque**: A delightful pastry filled with either almond cream or cherry jam, gâteau Basque has a buttery crust and a tender crumb. It's a popular dessert that showcases the region's love for sweets.

These Basque dishes reflect the region's rich culinary heritage and are sure to delight your taste buds!

Navarra's Specialties

Below are five Navarra specialties that you must try when exploring Northern Spain:

1. **Pimientos del Piquillo**: These sweet, roasted red peppers are a Navarra hallmark. Typically stuffed with a variety of fillings such as meat, seafood, or cheese, they offer a rich, smoky flavor and are often served with a drizzle of olive oil.

2. **Ternasco de Aragón**: This young lamb is renowned for its tender meat and mild flavor. Often roasted or grilled, it's seasoned simply with herbs and garlic, showcasing the natural taste of the lamb. It's a traditional dish for celebrations.

3. **Chistorra**: A popular street food, chistorra is a type of thin, spiced sausage made from minced pork and beef, flavored with garlic and paprika. It's often grilled and served in a sandwich or as part of a pintxo.

4. **Menestra de Verduras**: This vegetable medley features seasonal produce such as artichokes, peas, and asparagus, lightly sautéed and served as a side dish. It's fresh, colorful, and a great way to taste Navarra's rich agricultural heritage.

5. **Vino de Navarra**: The region's wines, especially those from the DO Navarra, are diverse, with fruity reds and crisp whites. A glass of local wine pairs beautifully with many traditional dishes, enhancing the flavors of the meal.

These Navarra specialties highlight the region's agricultural bounty and culinary traditions, making for a delicious culinary journey!

Wine and Cider Routes

Northern Spain is renowned for its exquisite wine and cider routes, particularly in the regions of Rioja, Navarra, and the Basque Country. Travelers can embark on immersive journeys through picturesque vineyards and lush landscapes, discovering the unique flavors and traditions of the area.

1. **Rioja Wine Route**: Explore historic wineries in towns like Haro and Laguardia. Enjoy guided tours that include tastings of exceptional red wines made from Tempranillo grapes, often paired with local cuisine.
2. **Navarra Wine Route**: Discover a delightful mix of wines, from robust reds to refreshing whites. Visit charming villages and sample local

delicacies, such as lamb and cheese, at family-run vineyards.

3. **Basque Cider Route**: Indulge in **Sidra**, the traditional Basque apple cider. Visit cider houses where you can taste the drink straight from the barrel, accompanied by regional dishes like a cod omelet.

4. **Scenic Landscapes**: All routes offer stunning scenery, with vineyards nestled among rolling hills and picturesque countryside, perfect for leisurely drives or bike rides.

5. **Local Festivals**: Experience vibrant local festivals celebrating wine and cider production, featuring tastings, traditional music, and culinary delights.

These routes promise an unforgettable experience filled with flavor and culture!

Best Markets and Food Tours

Here are some of the best markets, food festivals, and culinary tours in Northern Spain where you can dive into the region's rich culinary culture:

La Bretxa Market, San Sebastián

Visit this vibrant market in the heart of San Sebastián. You'll find fresh produce, local cheeses, and seafood. Don't miss the chance to sample pintxos at the bar section while interacting with friendly vendors.

Mercado de la Ribera, Bilbao

This iconic riverside market offers a wide range of local ingredients, from meats to fresh fish. Join a guided food tour here to taste regional dishes and learn about Basque culinary traditions from knowledgeable locals.

Pamplona Food Tours

Explore Pamplona with a local guide who will take you through historic streets, stopping at tapas bars and markets. Sample traditional pintxos and wines while hearing fascinating stories about the local food culture.

Haro Wine Festival

Experience the Haro Wine Festival in the Rioja region. This annual celebration features wine tastings, local food, and live music, providing a perfect opportunity to learn about wine production and enjoy culinary delights.

Cider Houses in Asturias

Visit traditional cider houses in Asturias where you can taste local cider paired with dishes like **chorizo** and **bacalao**. Learn about the cider-making process and enjoy a communal meal with locals.

Valle del Baztán Food Market

Discover the charming market in the Baztán Valley. Sample cheeses, cured meats, and traditional pastries while soaking in the picturesque scenery.

San Sebastián Gastronomika

Don't miss this prestigious food festival that attracts top chefs and food lovers. Participate in workshops, cooking demonstrations, and tastings to learn about modern Basque cuisine.

Bilbao Fiestas de las Sopas

Celebrate traditional soups at this unique festival in Bilbao. Enjoy tastings of various local soups while interacting with chefs showcasing their culinary skills.

Pintxos Tour in San Sebastián

Join a guided pintxos tour to visit several bars in the old town. You'll taste a variety of pintxos while learning about their history and preparation techniques from local chefs.

Mercado de San Antón, Madrid

While a bit outside Northern Spain, this market is worth a visit. Sample regional specialties, shop for local products, and dine at various food stalls while connecting with local vendors.

These experiences will allow you to savor Northern Spain's culinary treasures and connect with its vibrant food culture. Enjoy your culinary adventure!

Vegetarian and Vegan Options

When traveling in Northern Spain, you'll find plenty of delicious vegetarian and vegan options that cater to your dietary needs. In San Sebastián, visit **Kafe Botanika**, a cozy spot offering a range of vegan dishes, including seasonal salads and hearty grain bowls. In Bilbao, try **Vegan Munch**, where you can enjoy mouthwatering plant-based burgers and homemade desserts.

For gluten-free options, **Cafe Bar Bilbao** in the old town has a dedicated gluten-free menu featuring traditional pintxos made with care. If you're looking for halal choices, head to **Bocadillo**, where you can find flavorful wraps and rice dishes.

Don't miss regional specialties like **pimientos de padrón** (fried green peppers) and **menestra de**

verduras (vegetable medley), which are often prepared without meat. With these options, you'll be able to savor the rich flavors of Northern Spain while adhering to your dietary preferences!

Chapter 7

Activities and Outdoor Experiences

Hiking and Nature Walks

Hiking and nature walks in Northern Spain are your gateway to breathtaking landscapes, from rugged mountains to lush valleys. Popular spots like **Picos de Europa National Park** offer dramatic peaks and diverse wildlife, while the **Camino de Santiago** provides well-marked routes through stunning countryside. You'll also find beautiful coastal trails in the **Basque Country**, perfect for soaking in ocean views.

As you plan your adventures, remember to bring layered clothing—weather can change quickly—and always pack water and snacks. Consider visiting during the shoulder seasons for fewer crowds and milder conditions. Whether you're a beginner or an experienced hiker,

Northern Spain has incredible experiences waiting for you!

Camino de Santiago

Routes and Tips for Pilgrims

The **Camino de Santiago**, or the Way of St. James, is a historic pilgrimage that draws travelers seeking spiritual growth and adventure. With various routes to choose from, the most popular are the **Camino Francés**, starting in St. Jean Pied de Port, and the **Camino del Norte**, which follows the stunning northern coast. Here are some insider tips: plan your stages carefully, book your accommodation in advance during peak seasons, and invest in a good pair of walking shoes. Don't forget to carry a pilgrim's passport to collect stamps along the way. Whether you're walking for faith, reflection, or fitness, the Camino promises a transformative journey through breathtaking landscapes and rich history.

Beaches and Coastal Adventures

Northern Spain is home to some of the country's most stunning beaches and coastal adventures. From the famous **La Concha** in San Sebastián, known for its picturesque bay and vibrant promenade, to **Playa de la Victoria** in Cádiz, with its golden sands and lively atmosphere, you'll find a perfect spot to relax or soak up the sun. **Insider tips**: arrive early to snag a good spot, and try local seafood at beachside restaurants. Don't forget to explore hidden coves and participate in water sports like surfing or paddleboarding for an unforgettable coastal experience!

Surfing Spots

Zarautz, San Sebastián, and Somo

Northern Spain is a surfer's paradise, offering fantastic waves and stunning coastal scenery. Zarautz is famous for its long beach and consistent surf, making it ideal for both beginners and experienced surfers. San Sebastián boasts several surf spots, particularly Zurriola Beach, where you can catch great waves alongside a vibrant atmosphere. Somo, near Santander, is known for its sandy beach and less crowded waves, perfect for a more relaxed surfing experience. Insider tip: rent your gear from local shops to get the best advice and check the surf reports for optimal conditions. Grab your board and ride the waves!

Hidden Coves and Family-Friendly Beaches

Northern Spain is home to stunning hidden coves and family-friendly beaches, perfect for a relaxing day by the sea. **Playa de la Arnía** is a hidden gem near Santander, featuring dramatic cliffs and clear waters, ideal for exploring rock pools. For families, **Playa de la Concha** in San Sebastián offers calm waters and amenities like playgrounds and restaurants. Another great spot is **Playa de Gorliz**, which has shallow waters and soft sand, perfect for kids. **Insider tip**: arrive early to secure a good spot, and pack a picnic to enjoy a day of fun in the sun with your loved ones!

Festival and Events

San Fermín Festival (Pamplona)

This world-famous festival is celebrated in July and is best known for the thrilling Running of the Bulls. The festivities include parades, fireworks, and traditional music. **Time**: July 6-14 **Insider Tips**: Arrive early for the best viewing spots during the bull runs, and remember to wear white with a red scarf! Stay hydrated and pace yourself through the week of celebrations.

Semana Grande (Bilbao)

Known as the Big Week, this festival features concerts, street performances, and food stalls. It celebrates the city's patron saint with vibrant activities. **Time**: Late

August (exact dates vary) **Insider Tips**: Check the festival program in advance for events you don't want to miss. Bring cash for street food and enjoy the lively atmosphere with locals!

La Batalla de los Vino (Haro)

This unique wine festival in Haro involves a playful wine fight where participants douse each other with red wine. It's a fun way to celebrate local viticulture! **Time**: June 29 **Insider Tips**: Wear clothes you don't mind getting stained, and arrive early to secure a good spot for the wine bottle. Don't forget to enjoy local wines throughout the day!

Fiesta de San Isidro (Madrid)

Although primarily a Madrid festival, this celebration of the patron saint of farmers often features events in rural parts of Northern Spain. Expect traditional music, dancing, and food. **Time**: May 15 **Insider Tips**: Try the local dishes offered at the festival, and participate in the parades for an authentic experience.

Feria de Abril (Seville)

While this is a Seville festival, many people from Northern Spain attend. It features flamenco dancing, traditional costumes, and local cuisine. **Time**: Two weeks after Easter (dates vary) **Insider Tips**: Wear comfortable shoes for dancing, and arrive in traditional attire for a more immersive experience. Enjoy tapas at the casetas (temporary tents) for a taste of Andalusian culture.

Festival de la Sidra (Asturias)

Celebrate Asturias' cider culture with tastings, competitions, and traditional music. This festival showcases local producers and their delicious cider. **Time**: Early October **Insider Tips**: Participate in cider-pouring competitions to get a feel for the local tradition. Make sure to try traditional Asturian dishes alongside your cider!

Festival Internacional de Teatro Clásico (Almagro)

This classical theater festival celebrates Spanish and international plays in beautiful historical settings. It features performances, workshops, and talks. **Time:** July **Insider Tips**: Book your tickets in advance, as popular shows sell out quickly. Arrive early to enjoy the ambiance of the town before performances start.

Pintxos Festival (San Sebastián)

Experience the culinary delights of the Basque Country with a pintxos festival featuring local bars competing for the best pintxo. **Time:** Various dates throughout the year **Insider Tips**: Grab a festival map to guide you to participating bars. Be sure to sample as many pintxos as possible!

Festival de Jazz de San Sebastián

This renowned jazz festival brings together local and international musicians for an incredible celebration of music. **Time:** July **Insider Tips**: Book your tickets in advance for popular concerts. Explore local bars for more intimate jazz performances during the festival.

Fiesta de la Virgen Blanca (Vitoria-Gasteiz)

Celebrating the city's patron saint, this festival features music, parades, and fireworks, showcasing the vibrant culture of Vitoria-Gasteiz. **Time**: Early August **Insider Tips**: Join in the festivities by wearing traditional attire and participating in local dances. Arrive early for the best views of the parades!

These festivals and events offer a unique glimpse into the rich culture and traditions of Northern Spain. Enjoy the celebrations and immerse yourself in the local atmosphere!

Wildlife Watching

Bears, Wolves, and Birds in Natural Parks

Wildlife watching in Northern Spain offers an incredible opportunity to observe bears, wolves, and diverse bird species in their natural habitats. Head to **Picos de Europa National Park**, where you might spot the elusive Cantabrian brown bear and see breathtaking landscapes. **Somiedo Natural Park** is another great spot for wolf sightings, along with its rich biodiversity. For bird enthusiasts, the **Doñana National Park** is renowned for its vast array of migratory birds. **Insider tip**: Join guided tours for the best chances of sightings and to learn about the ecosystems. Bring binoculars and be patient—nature rewards those who wait!

Watersports

Kayaking, Sailing, and Paddleboarding

Watersports in Northern Spain offer thrilling adventures amid stunning coastal scenery. **San Sebastián** is a top spot for kayaking, where you can paddle around La Concha Bay while enjoying breathtaking views. **Zarautz** is perfect for surfing and paddleboarding, thanks to its consistent waves and beautiful beach. For sailing enthusiasts, the **Bay of Biscay** offers fantastic opportunities with various rental options available. **Insider tip**: Check local weather conditions and tides before heading out, and consider joining guided tours for a safer experience. Don't forget to pack sunscreen and water to stay hydrated during your aquatic adventures!

Chapter 8

Shopping and Souvernirs

The shopping scene in Northern Spain is vibrant and diverse, reflecting the region's rich culture and craftsmanship. In cities like San Sebastián and Bilbao, you'll find a mix of high-end boutiques, local artisan shops, and bustling markets. La Bretxa Market in San Sebastián offers fresh produce and traditional Basque products, while the Ribera Market in Bilbao showcases local delicacies. Look for unique items like handcrafted pottery, artisanal cheeses, and regional wines. The annual Sales (rebajas) season provides excellent discounts, making it a great time to explore the local shopping culture while picking up unique souvenirs!

What to Buy

Local Crafts, Textiles, and Ceramics

- **Basque Beret**: This traditional hat is both stylish and warm. You can find it in local shops in **San Sebastián**.
- **Ceramic Pottery**: Look for handcrafted pottery with vibrant colors, especially from **Talavera**. Markets in **Bilbao** are great places to shop.
- **Alpargatas (Espadrilles)**: These comfortable canvas shoes are perfect for summer. Check out local boutiques in **Pamplona** for a variety of styles.
- **Traditional Textiles**: Unique woven goods like tablecloths and blankets can be found in **Santander**.
- **Cheese (Idiazábal)**: Don't leave without trying this rich smoked sheep's cheese, available at markets in **La Rioja**.
- **Handmade Leather Goods**: From bags to wallets, you'll find excellent craftsmanship in shops in **Vitoria-Gasteiz**.

- **Cider (Sidra)**: Enjoy authentic Asturian cider, which you can buy fresh at cider houses in **Asturias**.
- **Pintxos Cookbooks**: Learn to recreate local tapas at home; these are available in bookstores throughout the Basque Country.
- **Local Wines**: Discover exceptional wines from the **Rioja** region at vineyard gift shops.
- **Handcrafted Jewelry**: Look for unique designs inspired by nature in artisan markets across **Bilbao**.

These items will not only enrich your travel experience but also provide a taste of Northern Spain's vibrant culture!

Best Shopping Streets and Markets

Here are some of the best shopping streets and markets in Northern Spain, where you can find unique, locally-made products:

Calle 31 de Agosto, San Sebastián

This charming street is lined with pintxos bars and artisan shops. You'll find beautifully crafted Basque berets, handmade jewelry, and local gourmet products like **Idiazábal cheese**. The vibrant atmosphere makes it perfect for leisurely shopping and tasting.

Mercado de la Ribera, Bilbao

This bustling market is a feast for the senses, featuring fresh produce, seafood, and traditional Basque delicacies. Look for locally-made pastries and artisanal cheeses. It's an excellent place to experience Basque culture while picking up unique food items.

Calle de la Estación, Vitoria-Gasteiz

This street is home to various boutiques selling handmade leather goods and traditional textiles. The unique craftsmanship reflects the region's artisanal heritage, making it a great spot for finding quality souvenirs.

Mercado de San Antón, Madrid

Although in Madrid, this market is worth a visit for its array of locally sourced products. Sample artisanal cheeses, cured meats, and wines. It's a great spot for foodies looking for authentic flavors.

Plaza del Mercado, Pamplona

Explore this lively market for fresh produce and local specialties. You'll find seasonal fruits, vegetables, and traditional dishes. The plaza also hosts local artisans selling handmade crafts, providing a glimpse into the region's culture.

Calle Mayor, Burgos

This picturesque street features a mix of shops offering traditional crafts, including pottery and textiles. You'll find unique items that showcase the rich history and craftsmanship of the region.

Calle de la Bolsa, Bilbao

For a more off-the-beaten-path experience, wander down this street, home to quirky shops selling vintage goods, antiques, and local artisan crafts. It's perfect for treasure hunting and discovering unique finds.

Plaza de la Virgen Blanca, Vitoria-Gasteiz

Visit this square to explore local artisan markets, especially during festivals. You'll find handmade crafts, local foods, and traditional clothing that reflect the area's cultural significance.

These shopping experiences not only offer unique products but also allow you to immerse yourself in the local culture and traditions of Northern Spain!

Wine and Food Gifts

From Cider to Jamón

Here are some fantastic wine and food gifts you can find in Northern Spain, perfect for sharing a taste of the region with friends and family:

Cider (Sidra)

Asturian cider is a unique gift, characterized by its slightly sour flavor and refreshing taste. Look for artisanal bottles from local cider houses, where you can find varieties that are traditional and organic.

Rioja Wine

A bottle of red wine from the Rioja region makes a perfect gift for wine lovers. Choose from renowned producers, and consider picking a vintage with a beautiful label to make it extra special.

Jamón Ibérico

This prized Spanish ham is renowned for its rich flavor and melt-in-your-mouth texture. Look for high-quality, locally sourced Jamón Ibérico, which can be vacuum-packed for easy transport.

Piquillo Peppers

These sweet, roasted red peppers from Navarra are often sold jarred and make a delicious addition to any meal. They can be enjoyed stuffed or as part of a tapas platter.

Cheese (Idiazábal)

Aged Idiazábal cheese, made from sheep's milk, has a distinct smoky flavor. This cheese is often wrapped in traditional cloth, making it a lovely gift for cheese enthusiasts.

Olive Oil

High-quality olive oil from the Basque Country or Navarra is a luxurious gift. Look for organic options with unique flavor profiles, ideal for drizzling over dishes or for use in cooking.

Chocolate

Artisan chocolate from local chocolatiers often features unique flavors, incorporating local ingredients. Look for beautifully packaged bars or gift boxes for a sweet touch.

Basque Pastries (Gâteau Basque)

These traditional cakes filled with cream or cherry jam make delightful gifts. Purchase them from local bakeries for authentic flavor.

Honey

Local honey, especially from wildflowers or chestnut trees, showcases the region's flora. It's perfect for sweetening tea or drizzling over yogurt.

10. Herb-infused Liqueurs

Liqueurs like **Pacharán**, made from sloe berries, are unique to the region. They make great gifts and are often beautifully bottled.

When selecting these gifts, look for local markets or specialty shops to ensure you're bringing home authentic flavors from Northern Spain!

Santiago's Craft Markets and Galician Pottery

Santiago de Compostela is a vibrant hub for craft markets and traditional Galician pottery, making it a fantastic destination for unique souvenirs. Here's what you can explore:

Santiago's Craft Markets

1. **Mercado de Abastos**: This bustling market is a must-visit for its array of local products, including fresh produce, seafood, and artisanal goods. You can find handmade crafts and gourmet food items that reflect Galician culture.

2. **Feria de Artesanía**: Held throughout the year, this artisan fair showcases the work of local craftsmen. Here, you can discover everything from jewelry to textiles, perfect for finding unique gifts.

3. **Pazo de San Lorenzo Market**: This market features stalls with handcrafted items, including

jewelry, leather goods, and home decor. It's an excellent spot to interact with local artisans and learn about their techniques.

Galician Pottery

Galician pottery is known for its distinct style and vibrant colors, often reflecting the region's natural beauty. Look for:

1. **Cerámica de Sargadelos**: This traditional pottery, known for its blue-and-white designs, is a significant cultural symbol. It's perfect for adding a touch of Galician artistry to your home.
2. **Barro de Gres**: This earthenware pottery is typically handmade and features rustic designs. You can find various items, from plates to decorative pieces, at local shops and markets.

Insider Tips

- **Bargaining**: Don't hesitate to negotiate prices at craft markets; it's part of the shopping experience.

- **Explore Side Streets**: Venture beyond main tourist areas to discover hidden shops and artisan studios.
- **Learn the Stories**: Engage with artisans to learn about their craft and the cultural significance behind their work.

Exploring Santiago's craft markets and Galician pottery will give you a deeper appreciation of the region's artistic heritage while providing you with memorable keepsakes!

Chapter 9

Family Travel in Northern Spain

Family travel in Northern Spain is an exciting adventure waiting for you and your kids! This region offers a perfect mix of stunning landscapes, charming towns, and delicious food that everyone will enjoy. Imagine exploring the breathtaking Picos de Europa National Park, relaxing on the beautiful beaches of the Basque coast, or wandering through the historic streets of cities like Bilbao and Santiago de Compostela. There are countless outdoor activities, engaging museums, and family-friendly attractions that will make your trip unforgettable. Get ready to create lasting memories as you discover the wonders of Northern Spain together!

Kid-Friendly Destinations and Attractions

Traveling with kids in Northern Spain can be a delightful experience, filled with fun and educational adventures. Here are five top kid-friendly destinations that will engage your little ones and make your family trip memorable!

1. **Parque de la Naturaleza de Cabárceno (Cabárceno Nature Park)** Located just outside of Santander, this wildlife park features over 150 species of animals in a natural setting. Kids can observe animals like bears, lions, and elephants up close. The park also offers activities like zip-lining and a cable car for stunning views. **Tip:** Plan your visit during the weekday to avoid crowds, and pack a picnic to enjoy in the designated areas. The best time to visit is spring and early fall when the weather is pleasant.

2. **The Aquarium of San Sebastián** This interactive aquarium showcases marine life from

the Cantabrian Sea and beyond. Kids will love the underwater tunnel that allows them to walk through a tank filled with sharks and rays. There are also touch pools for hands-on experiences. **Tip:** Check the schedule for feeding times to see the animals in action. Summer is the busiest season, so consider visiting in the shoulder months for fewer crowds.

3. **Sierra de Ancares Natural Park** Perfect for families who love outdoor activities, this park offers hiking trails suitable for all ages. Kids can explore lush forests and spot wildlife like deer and eagles. **Tip:** Join a guided tour for educational insights about the park's flora and fauna. Late spring and early fall are ideal for hiking, as the weather is mild and the trails are less crowded.

4. **Cabo Mayor Lighthouse and its Cliffs** This scenic spot near Santander features breathtaking views of the coastline and the iconic lighthouse. Families can enjoy a leisurely walk along the cliff paths, with plenty of photo opportunities. **Tip:**

Bring a kite for a fun afternoon; the coastal winds make it a perfect spot for flying kites. Visit in the late afternoon to catch a stunning sunset over the ocean.

5. **Picos de Europa National Park** A must-visit for nature-loving families, this national park offers numerous trails and cable cars that make the mountains accessible for children. Kids can enjoy picnics by the rivers and learn about the diverse wildlife. **Tip:** Consider visiting the Fuente Dé cable car for spectacular views. Summer is the peak season, but late spring or early autumn provides a quieter experience.

Each of these destinations promises fun and adventure for the whole family, ensuring that your trip to Northern Spain is filled with wonderful memories!

Family Beaches and Parks

Northern Spain offers a stunning array of family-friendly beaches and parks, perfect for creating unforgettable memories. Here are five top spots where your family can enjoy sun, sand, and nature!

1. **Playa de la Concha (San Sebastián)** This iconic beach is known for its golden sands and calm waters, making it ideal for families. Located in the heart of San Sebastián, the beach is equipped with playgrounds and beachside cafes. **Tip:** Arrive early to secure a good spot, especially during the summer months. The best time to visit is from late June to early September when the weather is warm and inviting.

2. **Parque de la Naturaleza de Cabárceno** This unique nature park, located just outside Santander, features both animal exhibits and beautiful green spaces. Families can enjoy picnics while watching animals roam in spacious enclosures. **Tip:** Wear comfortable shoes for walking and bring a stroller for younger kids. Visiting in spring or early fall is best for mild weather and fewer crowds.

3. **Playa de Famara (Lanzarote)** Although slightly off the northern coast, this stunning beach is worth a mention for its family-friendly vibe. With shallow waters, it's perfect for young swimmers, and the surrounding dunes offer opportunities for exploration. **Tip:** Bring beach toys and sunscreen, as there are limited facilities nearby. The best time to visit is in late spring or early fall for pleasant temperatures.

4. **Parque de los Picos de Europa** Nestled in the heart of the Picos de Europa National Park, this park offers breathtaking scenery and easy hiking trails suitable for families. Children can learn about local wildlife and enjoy outdoor activities like birdwatching. **Tip:** Pack a picnic and enjoy it in designated areas. Visit during late spring for blooming wildflowers and mild temperatures.

5. **Playa de la Magdalena (Santander)** This family-friendly beach is located next to the picturesque Palacio de la Magdalena. It features calm waters, golden sands, and plenty of space for

kids to play. The nearby park offers playgrounds and picnic areas. **Tip:** Check out the beach facilities for water sports if your family is adventurous. Late summer is ideal for warm weather and family activities.

Each of these locations offers something special for families, making them perfect for a day of fun and relaxation in Northern Spain!

Museums and Educational Activities for Children

Exploring museums and engaging in educational activities can be a fantastic way for families to learn while having fun. Northern Spain is home to several child-friendly museums that offer interactive exhibits and captivating experiences. Here are five top picks for your family adventure!

1. **Museo de los Dinosaurios (Salas)** Located in the quaint village of Salas, this museum showcases fascinating dinosaur fossils and life-size replicas. Kids can enjoy hands-on activities, making it an engaging experience. **Tip:** Allow plenty of time for the interactive exhibits. The best time to visit is during the warmer months when the surrounding nature is beautiful for a family walk.

2. **Museo del Ferrocarril de Asturias (Gijón)** This railway museum is perfect for young train enthusiasts. With numerous vintage locomotives and interactive displays, children can learn about the history of trains in a fun way. **Tip:** Check for special family events or workshops during your visit. Plan your trip for a weekday to avoid crowds, especially during school vacations.

3. **Museo Evaristo Valle (Gijón)** This art museum offers family-friendly activities, including art workshops for children. Set in a beautiful villa, the museum has a lovely garden

where kids can run and play. **Tip:** Visit on weekends when the workshops are often held. The spring and summer months are ideal for enjoying the garden.

4. **Oceanogràfic (Valencia)** Although not strictly in Northern Spain, this massive aquarium is worth the detour. Home to a variety of marine life, it features interactive exhibits where kids can learn about ocean ecosystems. **Tip:** Arrive early to enjoy the dolphin shows. Visit during the shoulder seasons (spring and fall) for fewer crowds and pleasant weather.

5. **Museo de Bellas Artes de Bilbao** This fine arts museum offers family tours and activities designed for children. The diverse collection ranges from medieval to contemporary art, sparking curiosity and creativity. **Tip:** Look for family tickets or free entry days. The best time to visit is during weekdays when it's less crowded, allowing for a more enjoyable experience.

These museums and activities offer excellent opportunities for your family to learn, explore, and bond while discovering the rich culture and history of Northern Spain!

Tips for Traveling with Kids

Traveling with kids can be a fantastic adventure, especially in the family-friendly regions of Northern Spain. Here are some essential tips to make your trip enjoyable for everyone.

1. **Where to Stay: Family-Friendly Accommodations** When searching for a place to stay, look for hotels or vacation rentals that cater to families. Many accommodations offer amenities like family rooms, kitchenettes, and kid-friendly activities. Websites like Airbnb and Booking.com allow you to filter for family-friendly properties, ensuring you find the perfect fit.

Consider staying in apartments or casas rurales for a more local experience.

2. **What to Do: Plan Kid-Centric Activities** Focus on destinations that offer engaging activities for children. Seek out interactive museums, parks, and beaches that provide opportunities for play and exploration. Coastal towns in Northern Spain often have family-friendly beaches with shallow waters, perfect for young swimmers.

3. **Pack Smart: Essentials for Kids** Always pack a travel bag with essentials like snacks, water bottles, and entertainment for long journeys. Lightweight games or books can keep your kids occupied during downtime. A portable first aid kit is also a smart addition.

4. **Be Flexible: Adapt to Your Kids' Needs** While it's great to have a plan, be prepared to adapt based on your children's energy levels and interests. Schedule downtime for relaxation and

feel free to explore spontaneous activities you discover along the way.

5. **Engage and Educate: Involve Your Kids** Encourage your kids to learn about the culture and history of the places you visit. Involve them in choosing activities and sites to see. This not only piques their interest but also creates lasting memories together. Enjoy your travels!

Chapter 10

Day Trips and Weekend Getaways

Day trips and weekend getaways in Northern Spain offer the perfect chance to explore stunning landscapes, charming towns, and rich cultural experiences without venturing too far from your base. Whether you're visiting for a short stay or want to escape the city for a couple of days, Northern Spain has something for everyone—from the picturesque coastline to lush mountains and historic villages. Pack your bags, grab your family or friends, and get ready to discover some of the best hidden gems the region has to offer!

From Bilbao: Rioja Wine Region and Gaztelugatxe

Rioja Wine Region

Description: The Rioja Wine Region, renowned for its world-class wines, boasts picturesque vineyards and charming towns. Here, you can tour wineries, learn about winemaking, and indulge in wine tastings. The region's rolling hills and scenic landscapes make it a delightful escape.

Distance & Travel Time: Located about 130 km from Bilbao, the drive takes approximately 1.5 to 2 hours.

Transportation: Renting a car is the most convenient way to explore the area, but you can also join organized tours that include transportation. Public buses are available but may take longer.

Attractions:

- **Bodegas (Wineries)**: Plan to visit 2-3 wineries (2-3 hours each) such as Bodegas Ysios and Marques de Riscal.
- **Haro**: Stroll through this charming town (1-2 hours), known for its wine festival and historic buildings.

- **Tasting Sessions**: Experience wine tastings at local bodegas (1 hour).

Gaztelugatxe

Description: Gaztelugatxe is a stunning islet featuring a picturesque chapel linked to the mainland by a winding stone bridge. Its dramatic cliffs and breathtaking views make it a must-visit.

Distance & Travel Time: About 35 km from Bilbao, the drive takes around 30-40 minutes.

Transportation: Driving is the easiest way to reach Gaztelugatxe, with parking available nearby. Alternatively, you can take a bus to Bakio and then a short taxi ride.

Attractions

- **Hiking to the Chapel**: The trail involves climbing 241 steps to reach the chapel (allow 1-2 hours round trip).

- **Views and Photography**: Spend time enjoying the panoramic views (30 minutes).
- **Bakio Beach**: Relax at this nearby beach (1-2 hours) if time allows.

Suggested Itinerary

1. Depart Bilbao early morning for the Rioja Wine Region.
2. Visit 2-3 wineries (10 AM - 1 PM).
3. Lunch in Haro (1 PM - 2 PM).
4. Explore Haro (2 PM - 3 PM).
5. Drive to Gaztelugatxe (3 PM - 4 PM).
6. Hike to the chapel and enjoy the views (4 PM - 5 PM).
7. Return to Bilbao by evening.

This itinerary offers a blend of wine tasting and scenic beauty, making for an unforgettable day trip!

From Santiago de Compostela: Rías Baixas and Lugo

Rías Baixas

Description: Rías Baixas is famous for its stunning coastal scenery, beautiful beaches, and delicious seafood. Known for Albariño wine, this region offers a delightful blend of natural beauty and gastronomic delights.

Distance & Travel Time: Approximately 75 km from Santiago, the drive takes about 1 to 1.5 hours.

Transportation: Renting a car provides the most flexibility, allowing you to explore at your own pace. Alternatively, you can take a bus from Santiago to towns like Sanxenxo or O Grove.

Attractions

- **Sanxenxo**: Enjoy the beaches and waterfront (2-3 hours).
- **O Grove**: Famous for its seafood, take a boat tour to explore the estuaries (2-3 hours).
- **Winery Visits**: Consider a tour of a local winery for Albariño tasting (1-2 hours).

Lugo

Description: Lugo is known for its well-preserved Roman walls, which are a UNESCO World Heritage Site. The city offers a mix of history, culture, and delicious local cuisine.

Distance & Travel Time: Lugo is about 100 km from Santiago, taking approximately 1.5 hours by car.

Transportation: The most efficient way to reach Lugo is by car. Buses are also available, offering direct routes from Santiago.

Attractions:

- **Roman Walls**: Walk the walls for stunning city views (1-2 hours).
- **Cathedral of Santa María**: Explore this architectural gem (1 hour).
- **Local Cuisine**: Enjoy traditional dishes at a local restaurant, such as pulpo a la gallega (1-2 hours).

Planning Tips

- **Timing**: Start early to make the most of your day.
- **Weather**: Check the forecast; Rías Baixas can be quite popular in summer, so arrive early to find parking.
- **Local Delicacies**: Don't miss trying the seafood in Rías Baixas and the local wines.

From San Sebastián: French Basque Country and Biarritz

French Basque Country

Description: The French Basque Country offers stunning landscapes, charming villages, and rich cultural heritage. Known for its unique blend of French and Spanish influences, this region is perfect for those looking to experience Basque culture across the border.

Distance & Travel Time: The French Basque Country is about 25 km from San Sebastián. Biarritz, a popular destination within this region, is approximately a 30-minute drive.

Transportation: The most convenient option is to drive, allowing you to explore at your own pace. Alternatively, regular buses connect San Sebastián to towns like Hondarribia and Biarritz.

Attractions:

- **Hondarribia**: This picturesque town features a medieval old town and stunning waterfront (2-3 hours).
- **St. Jean de Luz**: Enjoy the beautiful beaches and vibrant market (2-3 hours).
- **Biarritz**: Explore the iconic lighthouse and the famous Grande Plage (2-4 hours).

Biarritz

Description: Biarritz is known for its surf culture, elegant architecture, and luxurious atmosphere. This coastal city offers beautiful beaches, upscale shopping, and vibrant dining options.

Distance & Travel Time: Biarritz is about 38 km from San Sebastián, typically taking around 30-40 minutes by car.

Transportation: Driving is recommended for flexibility, but local buses also provide service between the two cities.

Attractions:

- **Biarritz Lighthouse**: Climb for panoramic views of the coastline (1 hour).
- **Côte des Basques Beach**: A popular spot for surfing and sunbathing (2-3 hours).
- **Ocean Museum**: Discover marine life exhibits (1-2 hours).
- **Dining**: Savor local cuisine at a seaside restaurant (1-2 hours).

Tip: Aim to visit during weekdays to avoid weekend crowds, and check local events for any festivals or markets.

From Oviedo: Cudillero and Covadonga Lakes

Cudillero

Description: Cudillero is a charming fishing village known for its colorful houses stacked on the hillside and its picturesque harbor. With narrow streets, seafood restaurants, and stunning ocean views, it's a perfect spot for a leisurely visit.

Distance & Travel Time: Cudillero is approximately 37 km from Oviedo, taking about 40 minutes by car.

Transportation: Driving is the most convenient option, but you can also reach Cudillero via a bus from Oviedo, which takes about 1 hour.

Attractions:

- **Cudillero Harbor**: Stroll around the vibrant waterfront and enjoy the local seafood (1-2 hours).

- **Mirador de la Garita**: A viewpoint offering breathtaking views of the village and coastline (30 minutes).
- **Church of San Pedro**: Visit this quaint church located on a hill for panoramic views (30 minutes).

Covadonga Lakes

Description: Nestled in the Picos de Europa National Park, Covadonga Lakes (Lagos de Covadonga) feature stunning glacial lakes surrounded by majestic mountains. It's an excellent destination for nature lovers and hikers.

Distance & Travel Time: Covadonga Lakes are about 80 km from Oviedo, taking roughly 1.5 hours by car.

Transportation: Driving is recommended due to limited public transport options. In peak season, a shuttle service runs from Covadonga to the lakes.

Attractions:

- **Lago Enol and Lago Ercina**: Explore these two picturesque lakes with walking trails around them (2-3 hours).
- **Covadonga Sanctuary**: Visit this historic site with a basilica and cave (1-2 hours).
- **Hiking Trails**: Enjoy numerous trails in the area, with varying levels of difficulty (2-4 hours depending on the trail).

With this itinerary, you can experience the best of both coastal charm and breathtaking natural beauty in a single day!

Chapter 11

Practical Travel Tips

Local Etiquette and Cultural Do's and Don'ts

Understanding local etiquette and cultural norms in Northern Spain can significantly enhance your travel experience. Being aware of these do's and don'ts will help you navigate social situations with ease and respect.

Local Etiquette and Cultural Do's and Don'ts

- **Do** greet people with a handshake or a friendly kiss on both cheeks.
- **Do** ask for local food recommendations and try regional dishes.
- **Do** maintain a moderate volume in public spaces; loud talking is often frowned upon.
- **Do** take your time during meals; dining is a leisurely experience.

- **Don't** rush through your meals; savor the flavors and the company.
- **Don't** interrupt conversations; wait for a natural pause to join in.
- **Don't** take photos in churches or religious sites without permission.

In conclusion, embracing these cultural nuances will not only show your respect for the local customs but also enrich your interactions with the people of Northern Spain. Enjoy your travels!

Safety Tips and Emergency Contacts in Northern Spain

Traveling in Northern Spain is generally safe, but it's always wise to be prepared. Here are some essential safety tips and important emergency contacts to keep in mind during your trip.

Safety Tips

- **Stay Aware of Your Surroundings**: Be mindful of your belongings, especially in crowded places like markets and public transport. Use a crossbody bag or a money belt to keep your valuables secure.
- **Follow Local Advice**: Pay attention to local guidelines, especially when hiking or visiting natural parks. Stick to marked trails and be aware of weather conditions.
- **Emergency Numbers**: The general emergency number in Spain is **112**. This number can be dialed for police, fire, or medical emergencies.
- **Health Precautions**: If you require medical assistance, look for the nearest pharmacy or health center. Pharmacies in Spain often carry basic medications and provide health advice.
- **Keep Copies of Important Documents**: Make photocopies of your passport, travel insurance, and other essential documents. Store these copies separately from the originals.

Emergency Contacts

- **Local Police**: 091 (for non-emergency assistance)
- **Ambulance Services**: 061
- **Fire Department**: 080

Local Hospital Contacts

1. **Asturias**
   - **Hospital Universitario Central de Asturias (Oviedo)**: +34 985 10 80 00
2. **Cantabria**
   - **Hospital Universitario Marqués de Valdecilla (Santander)**: +34 942 20 25 20
3. **Biscay (Bizkaia)**
   - **Hospital de Basurto (Bilbao)**: +34 944 00 60 00
4. **Gipuzkoa**
   - **Hospital de Donostia (San Sebastián)**: +34 943 00 70 00
5. **La Rioja**

- o Hospital San Pedro (Logroño): +34 941 29 80 00
6. **Navarra**
   - o **Complejo Hospitalario de Navarra (Pamplona)**: +34 848 42 22 22

By following these safety tips and keeping these contacts handy, you can enjoy a worry-free experience while exploring the beautiful landscapes and rich culture of Northern Spain!

Basic Spanish Language for Tourists

Knowing a few basic Spanish phrases can greatly enhance your travel experience in Northern Spain. Here's a handy guide to help you navigate conversations and interact with locals:

Greetings and Common Phrases

- **Hola** – Hello
- **Buenos días** – Good morning

- **Buenas tardes** – Good afternoon
- **Buenas noches** – Good evening / Good night
- **¿Cómo estás?** – How are you?
- **Estoy bien, gracias** – I'm fine, thank you.
- **Por favor** – Please
- **Gracias** – Thank you
- **De nada** – You're welcome
- **Disculpe** – Excuse me (to get someone's attention)
- **Lo siento** – I'm sorry

Asking for Help

- **¿Habla inglés?** – Do you speak English?
- **¿Puede ayudarme?** – Can you help me?
- **¿Dónde está...?** – Where is...?
- **¿Cuánto cuesta?** – How much does it cost?
- **¿A qué hora...?** – At what time...?

Dining and Shopping

- **La cuenta, por favor** – The bill, please.

- **Una mesa para (dos) personas** – A table for (two) people.
- **Me gustaría...** – I would like...
- **¿Qué me recomienda?** – What do you recommend?
- **¿Tienen opciones vegetarianas?** – Do you have vegetarian options?

Directions

- **A la derecha** – To the right
- **A la izquierda** – To the left
- **Todo recto** – Straight ahead
- **Cerca** – Near
- **Lejos** – Far

Conclusion

Familiarizing yourself with these basic phrases will help you feel more confident and engaged during your travels in Northern Spain. Don't hesitate to practice speaking; locals will appreciate your effort, and it can lead to memorable interactions! Enjoy your journey!

Sustainable and Responsible Tourism in Northern Spain

Traveling responsibly and sustainably is essential for preserving the beautiful landscapes and rich cultures of Northern Spain. Here are some tips to help you make a positive impact during your travels:

Choose Eco-Friendly Accommodations

- Opt for hotels, hostels, or vacation rentals that prioritize sustainability. Look for eco-certifications, such as the **Biosphere Responsible Tourism** badge, which indicates that they are committed to minimizing their environmental footprint.

Support Local Businesses

- Dine at local restaurants and shop at artisan markets to contribute to the local economy. Enjoy traditional dishes made with locally sourced ingredients and buy souvenirs that reflect the region's culture.

Use Public Transport or Walk

- Whenever possible, use public transport, walk, or bike to explore towns and cities. This not only reduces your carbon footprint but also allows you to experience the area more intimately.

Respect Natural Areas

- Follow marked trails when hiking, and avoid disturbing wildlife. Carry out any trash you bring in and stick to designated picnic areas to protect natural habitats.

Participate in Conservation Efforts

- Engage in local conservation projects, such as beach cleanups or wildlife monitoring programs. Many organizations welcome volunteer support, providing a unique way to connect with the community.

Educate Yourself and Others

- Learn about the local culture, customs, and environmental issues. Share your knowledge with fellow travelers to promote awareness and responsible practices.

By adopting sustainable and responsible tourism practices, you can help protect Northern Spain's stunning landscapes and vibrant cultures for future generations. Enjoy your travels while making a positive impact on the communities you visit!

Insider Tips from Locals for Traveling in Northern Spain

Traveling to Northern Spain offers a wealth of experiences, and who better to guide you than the locals? Here are some insider tips to help you make the most of your journey:

Embrace the Siesta

- Many shops and restaurants close in the afternoon for a siesta. Plan your schedule accordingly and take this time to relax or explore quieter attractions.

Try Pintxos

- In cities like San Sebastián, don't miss the pintxos culture! Visit local bars and try a variety of these small dishes, which are often displayed on the bar. Remember, it's customary to pay for your pintxos as you go.

Learn to Order Wine

- When ordering wine in the Rioja region, ask for a "tinto" (red) or "blanco" (white) and specify if you want a glass or a bottle. Don't hesitate to ask for recommendations; locals are proud of their wines!

Explore Lesser-Known Beaches

- While popular beaches like La Concha are stunning, locals often favor hidden gems like Playa de Langre or Playa de Gaztelugatxe for a quieter experience. Ask locals for their favorites!

Participate in Local Festivals

- If your visit coincides with a local festival, dive in! Events like La Semana Grande in Bilbao or the Fiestas de San Fermín in Pamplona offer vibrant celebrations with music, food, and culture.

Use Public Transport

- The public transport system is reliable and a great way to explore cities. Locals recommend using buses and trains to avoid parking hassles and enjoy scenic routes.

Don't Rush Your Meals

- Dining is a leisurely affair in Spain. Take your time to enjoy meals, and don't be surprised if dinner starts late, around 9 PM.

Learn Some Basic Phrases

- While many locals speak English, learning a few basic Spanish phrases can go a long way in enhancing your interactions and experiences.

With these insider tips from locals, you're set to have an authentic and enriching experience in Northern Spain. Engage with the culture, savor the flavors, and enjoy the beautiful landscapes as you explore this remarkable region!

Useful Websites and Travel Resources for Northern Spain

Having access to the right websites and travel resources can enhance your experience in Northern Spain, helping you navigate logistics, find attractions, and make the most of your trip. Here's a list of valuable resources:

Official Tourism Websites

- **Northern Spain Tourism**: northernspain.com
  - Provides comprehensive information about destinations, attractions, and travel tips.
- **Tourism in Asturias**: turismoasturias.es
  - Offers insights into Asturias, including cultural events, itineraries, and local cuisine.
- **Basque Country Tourism**: basquebusiness.com
  - Features information about the Basque Country, including attractions and activities.

Transport Resources

- **Renfe (Spanish Railways)**: renfe.com
  - For train schedules, ticket purchases, and travel planning across Spain.
- **ALSA**: alsa.es
  - Offers bus services throughout Northern Spain, with routes connecting major cities and towns.

Accommodation and Booking

- **Booking.com**: booking.com
  - Great for finding hotels, hostels, and vacation rentals throughout Northern Spain.
- **Airbnb**: airbnb.com
  - Perfect for discovering unique accommodations, including local stays.

Local Guides and Activities

- **GetYourGuide**: getyourguide.com
  - Offers a variety of tours and activities in Northern Spain, from wine tastings to guided city tours.
- **Viator**: viator.com
  - Provides options for booking excursions, tours, and activities tailored to your interests.

Travel Blogs and Forums

- **The Culture Trip**: theculturetrip.com

- Features articles on culture, food, and travel tips for Northern Spain.
- **TripAdvisor**: tripadvisor.com
  - A resource for reviews on attractions, restaurants, and accommodations from fellow travelers.

Language Resources

- **Duolingo**: duolingo.com
  - A fun way to learn basic Spanish phrases before your trip.

Utilizing these websites and travel resources will help you plan an unforgettable trip to Northern Spain. Whether you're looking for accommodation, transportation, or local experiences, these tools will make your journey smoother and more enjoyable!

Conclusion

As you wrap up your journey through Northern Spain, remember that this vibrant region offers a unique blend of stunning landscapes, rich cultural experiences, and warm hospitality. From the picturesque beaches of the Basque coast to the enchanting mountains of Asturias, every corner of Northern Spain has something special to offer.

Engage with the local culture, savor the delicious cuisine, and explore the charming towns and cities that make this region so captivating. Whether you're hiking the trails of the Picos de Europa, tasting world-class wines in Rioja, or wandering the streets of historic towns like Cudillero and Lugo, you'll create lasting memories.

By embracing sustainable travel practices and respecting local customs, you can enhance your experience and contribute positively to the communities you visit. Use the tips, resources, and insider knowledge shared in this guide to navigate your adventures with confidence and ease.

Enjoy every moment of your Northern Spain journey, and may it inspire future travels and discoveries! Safe travels!

Made in the USA
Columbia, SC
22 December 2024

50409638R00130